Cultivating Trauma-Informed Practice in Student Affairs

Offering a multi-tiered approach to supporting college students who have experienced trauma, this book considers how trauma manifests for post-secondary college students and how colleges and universities can implement trauma-informed practice in student affairs.

Author Tricia R. Shalka offers knowledge about trauma and its trajectories to help ground trauma-informed practice, before translating this knowledge into specific strategies that span a spectrum of individual and systems-level efforts in colleges and universities. The story of college student trauma is presented through several different lenses, including discussions around the research literature, what the author's research participants offer, and the author's own personal experience with trauma. Drawing on these diverse perspectives, Shalka initiates a journey of reflection and (re)connection that will ultimately inform an understanding of the challenges college student trauma survivors encounter and what it means to embrace trauma-informed approaches in student affairs supportive of student success and well-being-centric organizations.

Written in an approachable and conversational style, this book introduces new concepts to consider when working toward building a trauma-informed practice in student affairs and as such will assist student affairs practitioners, university administrators, and college-level educators in supporting students.

Tricia R. Shalka is an associate professor of higher education at the University of Rochester's Warner School of Education & Human Development, USA.

Cultivating Trauma-Informed Practice in Student Affairs

Tricia R. Shalka

Routledge
Taylor & Francis Group
NEW YORK AND LONDON

Designed cover image: © Getty Images

First published 2024
by Routledge
605 Third Avenue, New York, NY 10158

and by Routledge
4 Park Square, Milton Park, Abingdon, Oxon, OX14 4RN

Routledge is an imprint of the Taylor & Francis Group, an informa business

© 2024 Tricia R. Shalka

The right of Tricia R. Shalka to be identified as author of this work has been asserted in accordance with sections 77 and 78 of the Copyright, Designs and Patents Act 1988.

All rights reserved. No part of this book may be reprinted or reproduced or utilised in any form or by any electronic, mechanical, or other means, now known or hereafter invented, including photocopying and recording, or in any information storage or retrieval system, without permission in writing from the publishers.

Trademark notice: Product or corporate names may be trademarks or registered trademarks, and are used only for identification and explanation without intent to infringe.

Library of Congress Cataloging-in-Publication Data
Names: Shalka, Tricia R., author.
Title: Cultivating trauma-informed practice in student affairs/Tricia Shalka.
Description: New York, NY: Routledge, 2024. | Includes bibliographical references and index.
Identifiers: LCCN 2023021566 (print) | LCCN 2023021567 (ebook) | ISBN 9781642674606 (hardback) | ISBN 9781642674613 (paperback) | ISBN 9781003444435 (ebook)
Subjects: LCSH: Student affairs services—Administration. | Student affairs administrators—Training of. | Psychic trauma. | Student counselors—Training of. | College students—Mental health.
Classification: LCC LB2342.92. S53 2024 (print) | LCC LB2342.92 (ebook) | DDC 378.1/01—dc23/eng/20230511
LC record available at https://lccn.loc.gov/2023021566
LC ebook record available at https://lccn.loc.gov/2023021567

ISBN: 978-1-642-67460-6 (hbk)
ISBN: 978-1-642-67461-3 (pbk)
ISBN: 978-1-003-44443-5 (ebk)

DOI: 10.4324/9781003444435

Typeset in Adobe Caslon Pro
by Apex CoVantage, LLC

Contents

About the Author		vi
Prologue		vii
	Introduction	1
1	What Is Trauma?	4
2	What Might It Be Like for a College Student to Experience Trauma?	22
3	What Does It Mean to Be Trauma-Informed?	42
4	Personal Practices for Trauma-Informed Student Affairs Work	59
5	Supporting Students Who Have Experienced Trauma	83
6	Supporting Student Leaders Who Care for Others	109
7	The Organizational End Goal: Equity-Focused Systems of Wellness and Care	128
8	Toward a Trauma-Informed Student Affairs Practice	151
Index		156

About the Author

Tricia R. Shalka is an associate professor of higher education at the University of Rochester's Warner School of Education & Human Development. Her research has primarily investigated the impacts of traumatic experience(s) on college students in terms of their development, relationships, and navigations of campus environments. Dr. Shalka's scholarship also explores how trauma-informed practices can inform the work of both administrators and faculty in higher education. Her work has appeared in some of the top journals in higher education, and she has won several awards for her research and teaching. Prior to becoming a faculty member, Dr. Shalka spent several years working in higher education administration in areas such as residential life, fraternity and sorority life, institutional assessment, and development and alumni relations. She credits those experiences for actively shaping her scholarship and teaching. Dr. Shalka holds a PhD from the Ohio State University, an MA from the University of Maryland, and a BA from Dartmouth College.

Prologue

I never really understood the significance of May Day. I grew up in Canada and had heard the term, but that was about it. Then, during the spring of 2003 I was a sophomore college student studying abroad in Lyon, France, and became acutely aware of the holiday and its significance while trying to navigate traveling that May 1 in a country with a strong tradition of labor strikes. I was headed to the south of France on a trip with friends, and we'd been advised that rather than hopping on the metro (that was just a block from where I lived) to get to the main train station that we should leave *lots* of extra time to walk across much of the city to get there instead.

My walk to the train station that day is emblazoned in my mind in the same way that many events of that weekend are. That memory is stuck there not because the labor strike that weekend was unusual, because it wasn't. Instead, that weekend for me was a bit like the Robert Frost poem about coming across two roads in a wood and having to choose one direction and then looking back on it all with a self-congratulatory attitude as if you knew what you were doing at the time when you really didn't. In other words, that poem is about the ways we make meaning in retrospect and how things take on much more significance after the fact than they tend to when we're just living those mundane moments at the time.

Many of the events of that May Day weekend take on that heightened sense of importance and stay in my memory now not because they were that significant at the time, but rather because they became significant because of what happened at the end of that weekend. Before I went to bed the night of May 3 in Nîmes, I wrote in my journal as I often do when I'm traveling. The final sentence in that entry was: "Tomorrow will be a quiet day in Nîmes before returning to Lyon." That entry, too, would have been forgettable enough, but, again, retrospect imbues it with meaning. In many ways, that tomorrow didn't come for me and certainly not in the ways I had imagined it would. I would wake up later that night to the smell of smoke only to realize I was trapped inside a burning hotel. By the time I was rescued, I'd already sustained serious injuries and would be put to sleep and ultimately transferred to a specialized burn center in Montpellier.

My crash course in trauma had begun.

I share my trauma story here to help situate the work that I do and offer you a glimpse at the real person behind the words. My experience of trauma that began in Nîmes was terrifying and difficult and overwhelming. It was also enlightening, filled with love from amazing people, and sprinkled with grace. Ultimately, that experience propelled me onto a path that I would never have imagined, including the work I have engaged in for a decade now as a researcher of experiences of trauma among college students. In what follows, I tell the story of college student trauma through many lenses—what the research literature offers, what my research participants offer (whose names in this book are pseudonyms they selected), and what I've experienced personally. To those who are seeking to support students through trauma, it is my hope that this book will offer some concepts to think with in your work alongside survivors. To those who have been or are in the midst of navigating the ripples of traumatic experience, it is my hope that in what follows you will see aspects of yourself and find some moments of understanding, solace, and hope. No matter how you arrive at this conversation, you are not alone.

Introduction

Amira shared that being plus-sized and Muslim meant she consistently felt she stood out on her campus. Amira experienced several pervasive forms of trauma because of these identities, in addition to event-based examples of trauma including having her hijab ripped off her head as she walked to her car one night. Collectively, these traumatic experiences meant that Amira was in frequent states of anxiety moving through campus spaces and "[felt] like an outsider."

Liv lost a close friend from home to suicide part way through her sophomore year of college. In the hours, days and weeks that followed, Liv talked about increasingly feeling on the outside looking in. She described it as having outlived the collective experience of her friend group.

Paige felt something similar after leaving the Mormon church and having members of her family turn their backs on her. Rather than leaning on friends for support, Paige instead felt that they just wouldn't be able to understand. To continue feeling connected to her friends, Paige did something that suggests the opposite—she grew increasingly silent with them and didn't share how much she was struggling.

Over several years of talking to college student survivors[1] of trauma, I have learned that Amira's and Liv's and Paige's stories are sadly not uncommon. Many college students have experienced or will experience something traumatic in their lives. Yet, so many who have experienced trauma confront the realities of feeling like they are "out of the realm of . . . collective experience" as Liv would describe it. In interview after interview, I have heard survivors tell me their motivation for participating in my research was to share their stories and voices so other people like them might someday know they're not alone.

Social connection is wired into us as human beings. Yet, as sociologist Dr. Kai Erikson (1995) would remind us, "trauma has both centripetal and centrifugal tendencies" (p. 186). It can draw us closer to others as we lean on them for the empathetic support needed through recuperation. It can also draw us further away from the people we hold most dear, particularly when we feel that our traumatic experiences have pushed us beyond what can be understood by others.

This book is a call back to connection. One of the best ways that college student survivors of trauma can feel connected and understood in their college experiences is by being part of connected, empathetic communities where people understand what trauma is and how it might impact who survivors are in the world and how they relate to others. Trauma-informed practice is fundamentally about taking knowledge about trauma and its prevalence and then using that information to actively inform our policies, practices, and interactions. In the chapters that follow, I will offer knowledge about trauma and its trajectories to help ground what a trauma-informed practice in student affairs might begin with. I will then translate that knowledge into specific ways of being and strategies that we can engage in our student affairs practice that span a spectrum of individual and systems-level efforts.

In the pages that follow, I invite you on a journey of reflection and (re)connection through the stories of the many survivors of trauma who have shared their experiences with me. For those who are trying to be good supports for college student survivors of trauma, I hope these narratives will inform your understanding of the challenges survivors encounter along the way and how we can all be part of creating conditions for connection to fill the space of isolation.

Note

1 I use the terms *survivor* and *individual who has experienced trauma* (or similar terms) interchangeably throughout this book. I often use the term survivor as a shorthand, but simultaneously acknowledge and recognize that this may not be the term all individuals who have lived through trauma would use to name themselves.

Reference

Erikson, K. (1995). Notes on trauma and community. In C. Caruth (Ed.), *Trauma: Explorations in memory* (pp. 183–199). Johns Hopkins University Press.

1
What Is Trauma?

If you ask ten people "What is trauma?" you may get some similarities, but you'll also likely get ten nuanced responses to that question. Similarly, if you consult literature on the topic, you'll also get a wide range of answers about what constitutes a traumatic experience. I've asked my research participants how they conceptualize trauma and there are shades of similarity across their responses, yet there's equally nuance. In fact, what many researchers ultimately do agree upon about traumatic experience is that it's subjective. What is traumatic to one person may or may not be traumatic to another (Brown, 2008; Supin, 2016).

If there's no singular definition of trauma, why bother defining it? That is a complicated question that will mean different things at different times for someone who has lived through trauma. There may well be times when a definition isn't useful and is more limiting than helpful. On the other hand, there are times when naming something can be useful and perhaps even empowering. Claiming an experience as traumatic can sometimes help survivors know they're experiencing something others have also experienced and that they're not off-base to feel what they feel. Ultimately, definitions must be engaged mindfully.

During a commencement speech in 2015, Gloria Steinem recounted a story of being on a geology class field trip in college and watching a turtle crawling up to what she perceived to be a dangerous situation toward a road (Bennington College, 2015). She ultimately decided to "rescue" the turtle and return it to the nearby water only to then be told by her professor that the turtle had probably been struggling all month to reach that point to find a place to lay eggs and she had just derailed the whole operation. The lesson Steinem presents is "always ask the turtle." She goes on to offer the wisdom that the people living an experience are always more expert at it than those of us on the sidelines, even the supposed "experts."

In what follows, I offer some ideas to consider in terms of how we *might* think about traumatic experience and what *might* happen as responses to trauma. Know that similar to what Steinem offers, survivors themselves are ultimately the experts of their experiences. Some of what follows will capture one individual's experience well and not another's. As we work to build our collective knowledge about trauma and its ripple effects, it's critical to hold on to the reality that the only person who knows for sure what trauma is and what it looks and feels like in a specific situation is the person who has lived it.

How Might We Think About Traumatic Experience?

Trauma can be a slippery word to define in part because it means different things to different people. I asked one of my research participants, SJ, how she defines trauma and she gave a nod to definitional challenges by saying, "Gosh, I don't know. I don't know if there's one absolute way that you can define trauma. It's different for every person I would think." I appreciated her honesty in naming the difficulty of arriving at a singular definition. Many people have endeavored to define and name what trauma is in both research and practice, but the truth is the subjectivity of traumatic experience and the varied ways someone might react to a potentially traumatic event or experience makes a singular definition rather improbable.

Generally, I lean on definitions that are broad and inclusive, and often, I look to individuals themselves to name whether or not an experience is traumatic for them. Here are a few examples of how we might think about trauma in broad terms:

- The Substance Abuse and Mental Health Services Administration (SAMHSA, 2014) defines individual trauma as:

    resulting from an event, series of events, or set of circumstances that is experienced by an individual as physically or emotionally harmful or life threatening and that has lasting adverse effects on the individual's functioning and mental, physical, social, emotional, or spiritual well-being.

(p. 7)

- Author and trauma specialist Resmaa Menakem (2017) talks of trauma as a "wordless story our body tells itself about what is safe and what is a threat" (p. 8) and that anytime the body is overwhelmed by something that is "too much, too fast, or too soon" (p. 7) we can experience trauma. He shares that "we can have a trauma response to anything we perceive as a threat, not only to our physical safety, but to what we do, say, think, care about, believe in, or yearn for" (p. 7).
- Dr. Gabor Maté (physician and expert on trauma, addiction, and relationships between stress and healing) uses the analogy of a wound and scar to explain that trauma is:

a combination of a sensitive wound that if somebody touches it, it just triggers you and you hurt like crazy or if they touch scar tissue there's no feeling there. There's hardness. There's no flexibility. So trauma is a combination of extreme sensitivity and hardness.

(The Marianne Williamson Podcast, 2021)

In essence, our experiences of trauma create pain that we build protections around.

Many of the individuals I've talked to in my research studies have echoed similar broadness in working to define trauma:

- Violet shared that trauma could be "an experience, thought, or presence" that violates you. She also emphasized that it doesn't have to be something big and dramatic and, in her words, "it's something that's sometimes enduring and wears on you and your soul."
- Liv defined trauma as "anything that has a negative emotional impact that is disruptive to your everyday being."
- Lauren said she thinks of trauma as:

an experience that causes you a lot of pain. . . . [I]t's just an experience that's ingrained in your brain for sometimes your entire life, and it causes a lot of flashbacks, and an experience that you can't forget, because it was hurtful and devastating.

The definitions above provide some preliminary ideas about how we might think about trauma, but some additional specifics may also be useful. One initial way to break down some of these big definitions is to address the possible component parts of trauma. We can talk about trauma in terms of the thing(s) or circumstances that are potentially traumatic. We can also talk about trauma in terms of the responses that happen in relation to those things or circumstances, particularly traumatized responses. We can also talk about trauma as a multidimensional experience that implicates numerous aspects of our lives. Let's break down some of these component parts below.

Sources of Trauma

Trauma can be understood in terms of the thing itself that creates or causes trauma, and there are, unfortunately, a variety of sources of trauma in our world. In past literature, trauma has often been framed as an event. Potentially traumatic events (PTEs) are experiences that have the capacity to be psychologically traumatizing. The "potentially" part of the term signals the subjectivity of trauma and how a particular experience could be traumatizing to one person but not another. Schiraldi (2000) clusters PTEs into three broad categories: intentional human, unintentional human, and acts of nature/natural disasters. Traumas that are intentionally human occur because of deliberate human actions such as war, abuse, assault, and suicide. Trauma that occurs because of unintentional human actions includes things such as car accidents, industrial accidents, nuclear disasters, and surgical accidents. Finally, natural disasters include events like hurricanes, floods, life-threatening illnesses, and sudden deaths.

In sharing Schiraldi's (2000) list, however, I'm cognizant of the fact that it misses some important things about trauma including something one of my participants, Violet, explained in her quote that I shared earlier—trauma isn't always a huge, dramatic thing. It's important to leave space for the reality that even when we're talking about events that could be traumatic it doesn't always have to be something as big as a nuclear disaster or a war zone. Trauma occurs in many other moments, too. For example, trauma psychologist Dr. Laura Brown (2008) explains insidious trauma and how frequent attacks or microaggressions that individuals experience because of systems of oppression such as sexism, racism, classism, and ableism can also contribute to traumatic responses and threats to safety. Brown uses the metaphor of drops of acid on stone to capture this kind of "gradual and often imperceptible erosion of the psyche" (p. 104).

The event-based model of trauma is ultimately sorely incomplete. First, an event-based model might inadvertently lead us to think of trauma as a singular event, which is not always the case as many people may experience multiple forms of trauma and traumatization over the course of their lives. Second, it leaves out many other forms of trauma including those that are more insidious, pervasive, and/or identity-based. The container of event-based trauma doesn't really hold experiences of trauma that are the products of systems of power and oppression like racial trauma, intergenerational trauma, or historical trauma very well. It also doesn't account for many forms of identity-based trauma in which trauma happens because of the identities we hold. It also doesn't hold many ongoing forms of trauma that someone might experience from conditions such as homelessness or prolonged engagement in highly stressful environments. Thus, we need to hold space for trauma that occurs not just because of specific events, but also the kind that is ongoing, stretches across generations, and/or is experienced because of who we are in the world.

Responses to Trauma and Traumatization

Not every person who is exposed to a potentially traumatic experience will have a traumatic reaction, but some will. Enduring the ripples of traumatic experience and subsequent traumatization is a paradox in many ways. On the one hand, the way the body reacts to trauma is a perfectly normal and appropriate response, especially once we understand more of what happens in the body in relation to trauma. On the other hand, many survivors of trauma may feel overwhelmed and out of control in the throes of traumatization. As trauma psychiatrist

Bessel van der Kolk (2014) explains, "Intense and barely controllable urges and emotions make people feel crazy—and makes them feel they don't belong to the human race. . . . as a result, shame becomes the dominant emotion and hiding the truth the central preoccupation" (p. 67). In other words, experiencing what it feels like to endure traumatization can be incredibly alienating and isolating, especially when survivors don't understand why they're reacting in certain ways and it seems others aren't.

Similarly, people around a survivor may misinterpret or not understand what is happening and why the survivor is reacting as they are, because those people near the survivor may also lack an understanding of trauma. One of my research participants, Juan Carlos, spoke about the complexities of this reality alongside the stigma that exists about traumatic experience:

> There's a lot of negative stigma associated with trauma after the fact, after the event . . . like [the assumption that] people go crazy after the traumatic event. People are crazy. The traumatic experience isn't crazy, but how people react to it is what is crazy and that's the stigma associated with it. . . . I feel like some people might perceive it that way.

What Juan Carlos is speaking to is a challenge many survivors encounter when they feel like others don't quite understand what they're going through. He is pointing out the flaws of how we as a society sometimes view the problem with the individual as opposed to focusing on the trauma that underlies the response as the actual problem. Maya Angelou poignantly articulated that "when you know better, you do better" (OWN, 2011). I believe that holds true for traumatic experience. Knowledge about what can happen after trauma helps survivors and those around them to recognize the reactions as understandable.

Responses to trauma run the gamut. As a result, researchers and practitioners have found a variety of ways to talk about what responses to trauma may be like. One often-used phrase is that of *fight/flight/freeze* to communicate how the body might react in moments of event-based traumatic experiences (van der Kolk, 2014). Fundamentally, our bodies are oriented to trying to keep us alive. When we encounter threats to our survival, our bodies go into automatic response systems that may result in us trying to fight the threat, run away from the threat (flight), or immobilize (freeze) in the face of the threat. As van der Kolk (2014) explains, a hormone response in the body should bring this response to an end once the threat has passed, but sometimes traumatization means individuals may not experience a return to baseline. This is what individuals might experience in a particular kind of reaction to trauma, posttraumatic stress disorder (PTSD).

PTSD is a word that has somehow slipped into American vernacular in ways that are both good and bad. The good part may be that we have a general collective awareness of the possibility that trauma can negatively impact how we move through the world. The not-so-good parts are the myriad misconceptions about PTSD because it's a term that gets used without fully understanding what it is. The first important thing to know about PTSD is that it is just *one* possible reaction to a traumatic experience and certainly not the only one. The second important thing to know about PTSD is that it is a particular psychiatric diagnosis. The reason that is important is that it means it's a term that has specific criteria for someone to be named as experiencing PTSD. In other words, meeting the criteria for having PTSD can be useful in the sense of having a label to explain what someone might be experiencing or even having access to particular kinds of resources that can be useful for recovery. But (and this is a big but), not meeting the criteria for PTSD does not in any way mean a person is or is not struggling after trauma (Briere & Scott, 2015). PTSD criteria are restrictive in how trauma is defined, which means many people who may well experience trauma and perhaps even have symptoms similar to PTSD may not meet the criteria. Racial trauma is a type of trauma, for example, that traditional assessments for PTSD may not capture (Williams et al., 2021).

However, since PTSD is an often-used word in relation to trauma and is an experience that an estimated 6.8% of U.S. adults will encounter at some point (National Institute of Mental Health, n.d.), I want to spend a bit of time here explaining what it is. First of all, to experience PTSD, an individual has to have had a traumatic experience that fits a particular definition. In the *Diagnostic and Statistical Manual of Mental Disorders* (5th ed.; *DSM-5*; American Psychiatric Association

[APA], 2013), trauma is defined as: "Exposure to actual or threatened death, serious injury, or sexual violence" (the Posttraumatic Stress Disorder section). The definition goes on to include the fact that someone could experience this kind of trauma personally, witness it occurring to someone else, learn about a close family member or friend experiencing this kind of trauma, or experience repeated exposure to details of trauma often through one's work such as being a first responder. As you may gather, this definition accounts for certain kinds of trauma but perhaps not others.

Beyond meeting the definition of trauma as outlined in PTSD criteria, an individual also has to experience certain kinds of symptoms that fall into several different categories. The first category is that of intrusive symptoms, which essentially means that aspects of the trauma are re-appearing in the present. Flashbacks, disturbing and distressing memories, and dreams can all fall into this category. The second category of symptoms accounts for the reality that someone who has experienced trauma and is suffering from PTSD is trying to avoid anything that is associated with the trauma. This can include reminders of the trauma, feelings, and memories. The third category of symptoms is what is called "negative alterations in cognitions and mood associated with the traumatic event(s)" (APA, 2013, PTSD section). This includes many things related to thinking and feeling such as losing interest in engaging in various activities, feeling disconnected from others, not being able to experience positive emotions, or struggling to remember aspects of the traumatic experience. The final category of symptoms includes those that account for a changed reactivity in the world. This includes things like being hypervigilant, startling easily, having trouble sleeping or concentrating, and being easily irritated or angered.

Beyond PTSD criteria (and into more general ways to explain what might happen after traumatic experiences), others have talked more broadly about the idea of hyper- or hypo-arousal responses to trauma (Ogden et al., 2006). Levine (2010) talks of this reality in terms of survivors of trauma stuck between feeling too much or too little in their bodies. On the one hand, experiences of being traumatized may result in hyperarousal responses in which someone is quick to startle, emotionally reactive, hypervigilant, and disorganized in processing information (Ogden et al., 2006; van der Kolk, 2014). Over time, someone in the throes of hyperarousal states after trauma may appear reactive and defensive (Ogden et al., 2006).

I offer an example of what hyperarousal might look like through an example shared by one of my research participants, Mia. Mia felt a general sense of lack of safety in the world after trauma, especially while walking home at night. Her hypervigilance at night was closely connected to her traumatic experience in which she and her mom were pulled out of their car at a gas station one night and her mom was physically assaulted in the process. After that experience, Mia had a heightened alertness on her walks home from campus at night. She explained that she would always set a timer to ensure she left campus while there were still people around who would see her if something happened. She spoke of the nightly walk in the following way:

> I tend to look straight ahead and I speed walk really fast. Unless I see a car, then I'll stop and I'll look around for a little bit but then, yeah, I go back to speed walking. . . . I feel like if there's more students around I feel a little bit safer, but I still do the same thing that I was doing if there weren't a lot of students around 'cause I don't wanna get distracted.

In many ways, hyperarousal responses may be what we're more familiar with as a society and recognize after trauma. However, the opposite is also possible, in which a traumatized individual experiences hypoarousal responses. In this case an individual may feel an overall slowing of the body and its energy resources resulting in feeling numb to emotions and sensations, sluggish, and difficulties engaging in clear thinking. Prolonged experiences of hypoarousal may result in a traumatized individual appearing meek and compliant (Ogden et al., 2006).

One of my participants, Juan Carlos, spoke of the ways in which he became aware of his trauma when he couldn't focus on what he was reading. He would read something, and it just wouldn't sink in. He said the word that really encompassed everything for him at that time was numbness, which is a hypoarousal response. He talked about that experience in the following way:

I had never felt so weak in terms of numbness and weakness. That's the best way I can describe that traumatic manifestation. . . . It was terrible. Terrible. Oh my God, I never want to feel like that again.

Trauma can change how someone experiences stress. What this often means is that individuals who are traumatized operate at a higher baseline stress level and can more easily experience dysregulation (Ogden et al., 2006; Supin, 2016). van der Kolk (2014) observes that survivors of trauma move through the world with a different nervous system in which they're "focused on suppressing inner chaos, at the expense of spontaneous involvement in their lives" (p. 53). Thus, for people who are traumatized, their inner systems tend to be a bit more revved up and ready to go relative to those who have not experienced trauma. This revved-up state may mean there's a certain sense of ease and spontaneity that gets threatened. This may cause challenges in relationships when others don't quite understand why someone may be quick to react or seem to cling to control or predictability. That traumatized person may be quick to react because the higher baseline stress level means there's less additional weight needed to tip the scales. But, many survivors of trauma learn that they need to constantly explain that reality to others. As van der Kolk (2011) notes:

> Many traumatized people learn to tell a story of what happened, so that friends and relatives can understand why they are so frightened, angry, or out of control, but the real problem is that they do not feel safe inside—their own bodies have become booby-trapped.
>
> (p. xix)

Multidimensionality of Traumatic Experience

Sometimes trauma is classified in terms of two large umbrellas of experience: physical trauma (i.e., a trauma in which your physical body is injured or violated) and/or psychological trauma (i.e., a trauma that is harmful to or experienced at a psychological level). The reality, however, is that regardless of whether the origins of trauma may be physical or psychological, the ripples of trauma are multidimensional and impact us at numerous levels of experience simultaneously including the cellular, physical, psychological, relational, communal, and spiritual. As one of my research participants, Aria, so brilliantly put it, "trauma is anything that happens to you or that you experience in your life that fundamentally changes, well honestly, everything."

We know from plenty of research that trauma can change the physical elements and experiences of our bodies (Levine, 2010; Perry & Winfrey, 2021; van der Kolk, 2014). This seems to make sense when the sources of trauma may be physical in nature and someone is left with the injuries and scars as testaments of what they have endured. But whether physical or psychological, prolonged exposure to trauma or being stuck in the throes of traumatic responses and traumatization can alter the very nature of our bodies at a cellular level (Perry & Winfrey, 2021). For example, traumatic experiences and traumatization can alter neural connections and the ways our brains function.

Traumatic experiences might be processed cognitively as a survivor strives to make meaning of what happened or continues to happen. However, processing of trauma happens not just in our minds but also in our bodies, our emotions, our relationships, and our communities. A survivor might feel trauma in their body as aches, pains, and lethargy, even if the traumatic event was not physical in nature. Dr. Peter Levine (2010), a medical biophysicist whose work has focused on trauma as embodied, draws attention to how what we experience in our lives leaves imprints in our bodies—the way we carry ourselves, the way we move through the world, or even how we appear. While it may be either subtle or pronounced, as the title of van der Kolk's (2014) book reminds us *the body keeps the score*. We make meaning of trauma and experience trauma complexly in the body, whether cognitively, physically, emotionally, or spiritually.

Sometimes experiences of trauma are felt principally at an individual level, especially when the source of a particular kind of trauma is directed at an individual. However, whether trauma happens to one person or a broader community, traumatization is felt in the context of relationships, communities, societies, and even across generations. Survivors may feel the tug and pull of relationships as they navigate simultaneous feelings of needing to be close to others while also needing to push them away (Erikson, 1995; Shalka, 2019). Meanwhile, the people around survivors of trauma are also implicated in many cases because trauma impacts not just individuals but also the people around the individual who may themselves experience fear, worry, emotional pain and overwhelm, and sometimes struggle with what to do to support the survivor. Trauma also can explicitly harm entire communities and be carried and replicated across generations. Research has demonstrated this in numerous ways in terms of historical and intergenerational forms of trauma (DeAngelis, 2019; Gone et al., 2019).

Struggling With "Does It Count?"

As discussed at the start of the chapter, definitions can be both empowering and limiting. Every time we work to try to name something, we simultaneously name what it is not, even if subconsciously. Take the example of gender. If I try to create a definition for you of what it means to be a woman in American society, I'm inherently also telling you what a woman isn't. And in trying to explain to you what it means to be a woman in American society, you may well have further questions that are relevant, such as "Is it different to be a Black woman in the U.S. than a White woman?", "What is it like to be a trans* woman?", and "What is it like to be a woman who is a single mother?". In other words, the act of defining something is both important to understanding *and* inherently exclusionary. In the case of human experiences and identities, the act of defining experience is complicated because we are multidimensional and complex beings that aren't easily reduced into categories.

There are many similar issues in trying to name and categorize traumatic experiences. By virtue of saying what trauma is, we say what it isn't. That whole process can raise more questions than answers because the subjectivity of trauma and human experience, generally, means we must consider a variety of dimensions (such as social identities, previous experiences) in thinking about what trauma is. This gets complicated, and definitions and categories often don't handle complexity very well. The consequence of this is that definitions of trauma have a long history of both challenging the validity of traumatic experiences and leaving some people out from claiming trauma entirely. As one of my mentors, trauma scholar Dr. Maurice Stevens

(2016) says, "naming something 'trauma' does not always help, and it never only 'helps'" (p. 20).

Unfortunately, we live in a world that has long-standing traditions of contesting traumatic experiences. With the advent of train travel and ultimately train accidents, the concept of *railway spine* emerged in the 1860s at first to describe a post-traumatic response that was thought to have physical origins but later to describe what was believed to have psychological origins (Caplan, 1995). Regardless of how the condition was framed in the late 1800s, there remained members of both medical and legal communities who were convinced those afflicted by railway spine were malingerers who were trying to make money suing railroad companies. By the early twentieth century, the massive scale of tragedy during two world wars brought on investigations of concepts like *shell shock* and *traumatic neurosis* to try to explain what was happening to soldiers and veterans who were struggling with their wartime experiences (Herman, 2015). Despite recognition that these experiences were happening, soldiers suffering from shell shock were considered "at best a constitutionally inferior human being, at worst a malingerer and a coward" (Herman, 2015, p. 21). Psychological trauma received significant legitimization in 1980 when PTSD criteria were adopted. However, these criteria have continued to reinforce contestations of many forms of traumatic experience, particularly those that are products of systemic oppression. As Brown (2008) notes, PTSD criteria are:

> narrow enough to make some important sources of trauma invisible or unknowable. . . . Because many of these invisible traumas are related to a survivor's multiple identities, ignoring or invalidating these experiences diminishes empathy in general and cultural competence in particular.
>
> (p. 96)

What this history offers is some context in understanding how traumatization has been discounted and contested. Although we have come a long way into the current moment where many examples of traumatization are acknowledged and recognized, it is still the case that many other forms of trauma are pushed to the periphery and lack broad recognition as legitimate. Ultimately, the problem of narrow definitions is not simply that some are left out, but also that these boundaries are defined in the context of systems of power and oppression. As Stevens (2009) explains,

> notions of class, race, gender and sex have all been central to the formation of popular ideas about whose sensibilities can be disturbed by near-death experiences, whose civility can be upset by the horrific, and who can be overwhelmed by fear; who, in short, can be traumatized.
>
> (p. 2)

It is in this context that some survivors of trauma encounter questions of "Does it count?" Survivors have been called crazy or weak or doubted entirely. Over time, these collective mechanisms and processes create an ethos where those who have experienced trauma may feel like if they could just toughen up, they would be fine. Or they may be led to believe that other people wouldn't have the same experience going through the same things. Or, perhaps worst of all, survivors may believe they don't deserve to claim the title of trauma.

Some of that questioning of "Does it count?" is ultimately connected back to the narrow ways trauma may be defined. One of my participants, Natasha, noted that some of how we've societally decided to define trauma doesn't capture the entirety of traumatic experiences. She spoke of things like the TV show ER or major disasters like Hurricane Katrina or Sandy as evidence of what we've agreed upon as a society to constitute trauma, and while those are potentially traumatic, there are traumas beyond these examples. As she explained: "For everyone else that doesn't experience those things it's like they're not able to use that word, like the T-word doesn't account for them." This was particularly salient for Natasha whose traumas were connected to her experiences of the intersectional marginalization of sexism, racism, and ableism.

Even for individuals who have experienced versions of trauma that perhaps fit more neatly into an agreed-upon definition of trauma, it can still be a challenge to feel that one's own experience "counts." Sexual violence is a good example of this. In many cases, there is broad acceptance that sexual violence is a traumatizing experience. Still, broader social systems cast doubt on the legitimacy of survivors' experiences by creating scripts of what sexual violence looks like or doesn't, often making it difficult for some survivors to feel as though they fit in that box to claim their experience that way. One of my participants, Charlie, struggled with this reality, particularly in terms of how their college could understand their experience of sexual violence or not. Charlie explained it this way:

> The external experiences [of my institution] were kind of like, "Here's all these resources you should be using, and here's all these things we need to do. We support you," but it felt like in order to earn support (and it felt like I had to earn the support) was by having a narrative that fit. I very much was realizing, too, that my narrative was different than many folks in a college experience; because often times it's somebody hiding behind a bush, right? Then they jump out at you, and you get one of those blue lights, and then you're okay. That wasn't my experience.

There are many downstream effects of the "Does it count?" or "Does it fit?" conversation including challenges to a sense of belonging. Belonging is more than just something that feels good—it is a basic human need (Strayhorn, 2019). As human beings, we need to feel connected to others, included in social spaces, and that we matter to someone. Questions of "Does it count?" threaten to shake survivors' capacities to feel they belong, sometimes in the very spaces they need to feel connected in order to heal. One of my participants, Paige, posed a poignant and heartbreaking perspective to this by saying:

> I'm not sure if I could have put words to it at the time, but I think there was dissonance between, "Okay, maybe I have experienced trauma, but now with this definition I haven't so where do I fit in this? Have I gone through traumatic enough experiences to be able to use the word trauma? And to almost belong in that community and in that group, or am I diminishing other people's experiences if I claim the word trauma?" Because it wasn't as severe.
>
> So feeling like I was too broken in a lot of ways to fit in with my friends who haven't experienced things, but not sure if I was broken enough to fit in the way people who had experienced trauma, and I think just

navigating that. Whether or not I could put words to it just made me feel more isolated of, "I don't think I could tell this professor I've experienced trauma or share those things, because maybe I haven't and maybe I'm just a mess and there is no word for it."

Feelings of being too broken but not broken enough are feelings that implicate a sense of worth, value, and belonging. Ultimately, survivors need to feel connected to others and valued in social spaces as part of ongoing efforts toward recovery. As Paige captured, that path isn't necessarily linear or straightforward.

Conclusion

I want to end here where I began—trauma is subjective. Definitions can be helpful, but definitions are also inherently exclusionary. Sometimes, it may be easy for those who have experienced trauma to see themselves within the boundaries of a particular definition of trauma, and sometimes that fit feels uneasy or unreachable. Ultimately, survivors themselves are the experts of their own experiences. They know what has happened to them. They know what they have endured. They know how that past shows up in their present. They are worthy. They are whole.

References

American Psychiatric Association. (2013). *Diagnostic and statistical manual of mental disorders* (5th ed.). APA. https://doi.org/10.1176/appi.books.9780890425596

Bennington College. (2015, June 7). *Gloria Steinem addresses the 2015 graduating class* [Video]. YouTube. https://www.youtube.com/watch?v=zAQDcl6Rs6Y

Briere, J. N., & Scott, C. (2015). *Principles of trauma therapy: A guide to symptoms, evaluation, and treatment* (2nd ed., DSM-5 update). Sage Publications.

Brown, L. S. (2008). *Cultural competence in trauma therapy: Beyond the flashback.* APA.

Caplan, E. M. (1995). Trains, brains, and sprains: Railway spine and the origins of psychoneuroses. *Bulletin of the History of Medicine, 69*(3), 387–419.

DeAngelis, T. (2019). The legacy of trauma. *Monitor on Psychology, 50*(2). http://www.apa.org/monitor/2019/02/legacy-trauma

Erikson, K. (1995). Notes on trauma and community. In C. Caruth (Ed.), *Trauma: Explorations in memory* (pp. 183–199). Johns Hopkins University Press.

Gone, J. P., Hartmann, W. E., Pomerville, A., Wendt, D. C., Klem, S. H., & Burrage, R. L. (2019). The impact of historical trauma on health outcomes for Indigenous populations in the USA and Canada: A systematic review. *American Psychologist, 74*(1), 20–35. http://dx.doi.org/10.1037/amp0000338

Herman, J. L. (2015). *Trauma and recovery: The aftermath of violence—from domestic abuse to political terror.* Basic Books.

Levine, P. A. (2010). *In an unspoken voice: How the body releases trauma and restores goodness.* North Atlantic Books.

The Marianne Williamson Podcast. (2021, March 25). *Understanding trauma: A conversation with Dr. Gabor Maté* [Video]. YouTube. https://www.youtube.com/watch?v=SUXVXD4m_4o

Menakem, R. (2017). *My grandmother's hands: Racialized trauma and the pathway to mending our hearts and bodies.* Central Recovery Press.

National Institute of Mental Health. (n.d.). *Post-traumatic stress disorder (PTSD).* https://www.nimh.nih.gov/health/statistics/post-traumatic-stress-disorder-ptsd.shtml

Ogden, P., Minton, K., & Pain, C. (2006). *Trauma and the body: A sensorimotor approach to psychotherapy.* W. W. Norton & Company.

OWN. (2011, October 19). *The powerful lesson Maya Angelou taught Oprah* [Video]. https://www.oprah.com/oprahs-lifeclass/the-powerful-lesson-maya-angelou-taught-oprah-video

Perry, B. D., & Winfrey, O. (2021). *What happened to you? Conversations on trauma, resilience, and healing.* Flatiron Books.

Schiraldi, G. R. (2000). *The post-traumatic stress disorder sourcebook: A guide to healing, recovery, and growth.* Lowell House.

Shalka, T. R. (2019). Trauma and the interpersonal landscape: Developmental tasks of the relational self identity site. *Journal of College Student Development, 60*(1), 35–51. https://doi.org/10.1353/csd.2019.0002

Stevens, M. E. (2009). From the past imperfect: Towards a critical trauma theory. *Letters: The Semiannual Newsletter of the Robert Penn Warren Center for the Humanities, 17*(2), 1–5.

Stevens, M. E. (2016). Trauma is as trauma does: The politics of affect in catastrophic times. In M. J. Casper & E. Wertheimer (Eds.), *Critical trauma studies: Understanding violence, conflict and memory in everyday life* (pp. 19–36). New York University Press.

Strayhorn, T. L. (2019). *College students' sense of belonging: A key to educational success for all students* (2nd ed.). Routledge.

Substance Abuse and Mental Health Services Administration [SAMHSA]. (2014). *SAMHSA's concept of trauma and guidance for a trauma-informed approach* (HHS Publication No. (SMA) 14-4884). Substance Abuse and

Mental Health Services Administration. https://ncsacw.samhsa.gov/userfiles/files/SAMHSA_Trauma.pdf

Supin, J. (2016, November). The long shadow: Bruce Perry on the lingering effects of childhood trauma. *The Sun*. https://www.thesunmagazine.org/issues/491/the-long-shadow

van der Kolk, B. A. (2011). Introduction. In D. Emerson & E. Hopper (Eds.), *Overcoming trauma through yoga: Reclaiming your body* (pp. xvii-xxiv). North Atlantic Books.

van der Kolk, B. A. (2014). *The body keeps the score: Brain, mind, and body in the healing of trauma*. Viking.

Williams, M. T., Haeny, A. M., & Homes, S. C. (2021). Posttraumatic stress disorder and racial trauma. *PTSD Research Quarterly*, *32*(1), 1–9.

2
WHAT MIGHT IT BE LIKE FOR A COLLEGE STUDENT TO EXPERIENCE TRAUMA?

Part of the work we're trying to do in a trauma-informed system is empathy—trying to understand what those who have lived through trauma are experiencing and feeling. Yet, empathy is nuanced and complex, especially when we consider how to understand someone's experience without being clouded by our own, a complexity captured by Brené Brown in a recent interview (Oprah Daily, 2021):

> The idea of walking in someone else's shoes and trying to understand what they're feeling, I believe, has no merit. I think the call is much more difficult and much more powerful—and that is to ask the person for their story of what it's like in their shoes and to believe them.

Comparable to what Brown describes, the kind of empathy we're aspiring to in a trauma-informed system is not just imagining someone's experience, but actually listening to their experience and believing it. Similar to the turtle story in the previous chapter, it's about listening to and believing survivors of trauma as experts of their own experiences.

It seems simple, but it's not in practice. As I reflect on what I've learned from college student survivors of trauma over the years, I know they also know it's not that simple, because they've often been the beneficiaries of having people around them who ultimately weren't able to empathize with their experiences. Part of that challenge may be because stories of trauma are difficult to hear and sit with, especially if we embrace these experiences not just as stories, but as real things that have happened to people we care about (Okello & Shalka, 2022).

But, if we can't listen, we also can't really know what a survivor is confronting.

When I asked one of my research participants, SJ, if she felt that people around her understood her experience of trauma, she answered with a conclusive "definitely not." In fact, SJ felt there were very few people she could open up to about her experience of sexual assault in college and it took her a long time to find even those few that she felt could safely hold her experiences. As we talked about the phenomenon of people not being able to understand her traumatic experience, SJ shared an important truism about trauma: "I feel like trauma is a big elephant in the room that people just don't talk about."

For a variety of reasons, many individuals' experiences of trauma are complicated by silencing systems that operate at both micro and macro levels (Herman, 2015; van der Kolk, 2014). At a micro level, I've witnessed many conversations over the years where a person musters the courage to open up about something traumatic in their lives and the listener responds with some version of waving their hands back and forth in front of their body to denote a "no-no" and says something like, "Oh that's ok. You don't have to tell me." I believe the listeners in these scenarios often convinced themselves it would be too hard for the person who experienced trauma to talk about it, so they are sparing the survivor having to share those difficult details. Right behind that breath, though (even if subconsciously), I think the listeners are often reacting to their own discomfort related to what hearing trauma narratives may emotionally activate in themselves. What's the impact of such a seemingly small moment for the person who has lived through trauma? To that survivor, the message is clear: *Who they are and what they have experienced is too much for others.* The effect of that message is silencing. It clearly communicates that the survivor's experience is not to be spoken, not to be brought into the social order, because the social order can't sit with it. If it can't be heard, it also can't be believed.

Silencing happens in macro and systemic ways too. Victim blaming is one of these processes where rather than being able to hold space for the reality that trauma has occurred, social mechanisms convince us that the person harmed is the person at fault. Again, the result for the survivor is one of silencing. The reality and details of their story become secondary to the blame and shame that is inflicted upon them. Individual acts of victim blaming reinforce broader social silencing, because then those who have endured similar traumas get messages that it's equally unsafe for them to bring their stories forward for fear of the narrative being turned against them in similar ways. This is a persistent issue underpinning sexual violence.

Collectively, micro and macro mechanisms of silence add to the landscape of what SJ described in terms of trauma being the elephant that nobody wants to talk about. Yet, the only way forward in supporting students who have experienced trauma is to engage mindfully with our own discomforts and work to educate ourselves and understand just what it might be like for college students to experience trauma. That work is ultimately what can bolster us in finding ways to "cultivate the courage to listen to the testimonies of survivors" (van der Kolk, 2014, p. 195) that is at the heart of being good support for those who have endured trauma. In that listening, we can then do the true empathetic work of believing what student survivors are sharing with us.

In this chapter, I offer several *possibilities* of what college student survivors of trauma might experience as ways to help attune ourselves to be better listeners for what college student survivors might be enduring. It is important to emphasize the possibilities part of this, because as I explained in the previous chapter, although there are many common features of traumatic experience, trauma is also inherently subjective and two individuals experiencing the same thing may have very different reactions.

What Do We Need to Be Aware of About Trauma in the Lives of College Students?

Research indicates that approximately 66% of matriculating college students have already had exposure to trauma and 9% of those new students will also meet the criteria for PTSD, signaling significant negative impacts and challenges to their experiences (Read et al., 2011). We also know from research that the childhood traumas that individuals carry with them can continue to ripple across the lifespan compromising an individual's health, development, and learning

(Felitti et al., 1998; Perry & Winfrey, 2021). For some, dealing with the adversity of traumatic experiences may mean not just challenge but also growth (Kilmer, 2014). What this all translates to is that students frequently arrive to college already carrying traumatic experiences with them that will shape the nature of their educational journeys. During the college years, some students who are already survivors of trauma will encounter additional traumas, and some additional students will experience trauma for the first time. Although college student experiences of trauma share commonalities with the kinds of experiences that any survivor of trauma will have, there are also a variety of contextual elements about the college years that create unique conditions for how students may experience trauma.

In 2019, 74.5% of undergraduates enrolled in U.S. postsecondary institutions were 24 and under, and 84.3% were under the age of 30 (U.S. Department of Education, National Center for Education Statistics, 2020). While these statistics certainly demonstrate that not all undergraduates are what we might consider to be "traditionally aged" or in the period of emerging adulthood, the vast majority are. This information is useful in recognizing that many college students who have experienced trauma in the past or are experiencing it currently are doing so while simultaneously navigating many important developmental milestones of early adulthood. For example, we know the period of emerging adulthood (that Arnett [2015] identifies as occurring roughly between ages 18 and 29) is a rich time for identity development and some of those fundamental questions of "Who am I?" (Arnett, 2006; Baxter Magolda, 2009). Early adulthood is a time of instability and feeling caught "in between" (Arnett, 2006), as well as a period in which individuals are experimenting with and gaining a clarity of internal voice that might be described as self-authorship (Baxter Magolda, 2009). Finally, early adulthood is also a time of significant cognitive development. Some have described this development as qualitative changes that may occur in terms of increased cognitive complexity toward capacities to discern nuance and subjectivity (Perry, 1968), while other bodies of research have illuminated the very concrete realities that the prefrontal cortex of our brains is not fully developed until around age 30 (Blimling, 2013).

In addition to the noteworthy developmental contexts underpinning how college students experience trauma, we also have to be attentive to some of the unique organizational and institutional factors that shape students' experiences. For example, while college students may have exposure to any number of traumatic experiences, some may be particularly prominent or visible in college spaces, such as sexual violence or racial trauma. Although we frequently approach student trauma from reactive stances in which we imagine trauma is somehow external to our institutions, we must recognize that our organizational practices, policies, and climates are also sources of trauma (Shalka, 2022a). In other words, students can be exposed to trauma and traumatized due to the conditions we have specifically created in higher education organizations.

When we're thinking about what it's like to be a college student experiencing trauma, we must be attentive to how trauma shows up in context. In what follows, I will offer some additional texture to what that might mean for college student survivors of trauma.

External Forces Shaping College Student Experiences of Trauma

Sometimes, trauma is falsely understood as a "problem" of the individual. That assessment is inaccurate for varied reasons. As I mentioned in the previous chapter, there is a multidimensionality to trauma that frequently means trauma is experienced in relationships and in relation to the contexts of which we're a part. In short, individual experiences of trauma aren't just about the individual—they are simultaneously about the external world pushing into and rubbing up against individual traumatic encounters. While individuals' experiences of trauma may impact others, individuals' experiences of trauma are simultaneously shaped by the relationships, communities, and contexts of which those survivors are a part. Let me explain that further by illustrating how external forces such as systems of privilege and oppression, social discourses, and social constructions of identity intersect individual experiences of trauma.

Privilege and Oppression

Trauma maintains an intricate connection to systems of power and oppression. At one level, many forms of trauma are caused by oppression (Venet, 2021). Race-based trauma, sexual violence, hate-based violence, intergenerational trauma, and historical trauma are examples of potentially traumatic experiences that are directly caused by systems of oppression that organize our social spaces. Notably, while any of these systems can be sources of trauma, the oppressive systems themselves can then additionally complicate how a survivor may experience their trauma. For example, research supports the connection between racism and trauma (Comas-Días et al., 2019). However, the impacts of racial trauma are not fully embraced in all spaces, which is in part a product of how dominant conceptualizations of trauma are rooted in White, Eurocentric renderings (Brown, 2008; Comas-Días et al., 2019; Hernández-Wolfe, 2013). The result means that a student experiencing negative impacts of racial trauma may find their experiences further complicated by not having their trauma fully recognized or understood. I believe this was some of what one of my participants, Natasha, was communicating in sharing that she was not the "poster child for trauma." Natasha's traumatic experiences were at the nexus of multiple marginalities of sexism, racism, and ableism. As a Black woman (one of the very few) at a competitive music school, her experiences of trauma were compounded because they were not easily visible to others in this climate in the ways other traumas may be more readily understood.

In other cases, even if the trauma itself is not as intimately tied to systems of sexism, racism, classism, ableism, etc., traumatic experience can be amplified at the intersection of any of these -isms. For example, one of my participants, Tyler, experienced a generally agreed-upon traumatic event in college—a car accident. There's nothing in how Tyler shared his trauma narrative with me that would indicate systems of privilege and oppression played any role in creating that traumatic moment. However, Tyler's recovery was certainly shaped by these systems including ableism and hegemonic masculinity. Tyler struggled in many ways in his recovery rubbing up against how these systems operate. Ableism was a salient feature in his narrative, as he grappled with feeling inferior and less capable as a leader because of his physical injuries and his persistent concerns about how others were viewing him. He shared an example of his struggle as a fraternity president during this time and trying to balance how to be seen as a legitimate leader:

> how do you mitigate being vulnerable, being a leader, and then also trying to also be your old self, if you will, where people don't view you as just handicapped? I couldn't go down to get to the meeting room in [my fraternity], people had to carry me down to the basement, and carry me to the chair. That was partially humiliating. It was like, here I am, still trying, but now I'm being carried by another twenty, twenty-two-year-old person.

A system of ableism created a sense of what constitutes "normal" and "not normal" for Tyler, and for many other survivors, I've talked to over the years. As Tyler's example illustrates, traumatic recovery isn't just about the trauma itself. It is also about these inflection points that arise in the context of systems of privilege.

Social Discourses

We're all embedded within particular social and cultural groups. Within these groupings, (whether a group of friends or social norms that guide societies), there are implicit and explicit messages that influence our behaviors. What this means in traumatic experience is that when a survivor endures something traumatic, that experience is already situated within a variety of discourses and norms about the meaning of that kind of experience.

Let me illustrate what I mean through an example. As a first-year student, SJ was in a women and gender studies course. Partway through a class session, another student publicly revealed they had been sexually assaulted. SJ interpreted that as an act of courage. Later, when the class split up into small group work, SJ was confronted by a peer's different interpretation. SJ explained it this way:

One of the group members that I had. . . . She was like "gosh that girl just wanted attention, like why would she just put it out there, that's not something that you talk about, like just out in the open like that."

SJ told me that story in relation to a follow-up question I had for her after she told me she was worried sharing her own trauma would upset people or ruin someone's day. Do you see what happened there? SJ's experience of sexual assault happened during her sophomore year of college. That encounter in class the previous year was still deeply embedded in SJ, and led her to believe others might perceive her as being attention-seeking too if she were to share her own experience of sexual assault. That kind of silencing isn't just a quirk of this one encounter in a class session for someone like SJ—researchers and clinicians have documented silencing systems that exist around trauma (Brison, 2002; Herman, 2015). As mentioned at the start of this chapter, that silencing can happen in micro ways as well as those that are more deeply embedded in the fabric of our social systems and discourses.

In addition to silencing systems, there are also many discourses of survivors needing to prove their victimhood. Discussions about what "counts" as trauma or not bring us into this terrain and are especially problematic given the often Eurocentric renderings of trauma in American contexts (Comas-Días et al., 2019; Hernández-Wolfe, 2013). Narratives of survivors needing to just "pull themselves up by the bootstraps" or "get over it" or "get back to normal" also inflict further harm and damage. This was the underlying logic of a professor who was baffled when one of my participants, Robin, was expressing why she struggled the night before an exam given her ongoing challenges of grief and trauma after her dad's death. "That was two months ago," the professor uttered in response to Robin's request for understanding. The implication to Robin was clear and damaging—she should be over it by now. Our language and normed ways of being in relation to one another can be deeply challenging in the face of trauma.

Social Constructions of Identity

Many student affairs educators are aware of the socially constructed nature of many group identities that we hold. What race or gender, for example, means in one social context may be different in others. These identities take on meaning in relation to others and the groups of which we are a part. They are made meaningful in the context of social interactions and the systems of privilege and oppression that serve as organizing frameworks for our lives.

Trauma literature has investigated how various social identities shape traumatic experiences. For example, studies have documented differences between men and women in terms of traumatic experiences, with women more likely to experience PTSD (e.g., Breslau, 2009). However, there are some real limitations to these kinds of investigations, as they stay at the level of describing differences, but don't tell us very much about the socially constructed elements of these identity categories that make experiences of trauma meaningful in particular ways.

Something I've learned in my research is how social norms about what various social identities mean can powerfully shape the experiences survivors have in relation to their trauma. Let's continue with the example of gender. In U.S. society, there are mechanisms that both explicitly and implicitly tend to privilege and favor being a cisgender man, often in terms of expectations of hegemonic masculinity (Brown, 2008; Johnson, 2014). I've found that these gender norms that privilege these forms of masculinity ultimately create challenges in many ways for survivors of trauma in their recovery. Specifically, I have seen examples of cisgender men and women in my previous studies sharing that they felt they couldn't authentically express their trauma for fears of being perceived as weak. For Tyler, this was a dominant theme after sustaining physical injuries and battling what he described as "a complex battle of what is it to be a man versus now as society sees me, 'a crippled guy'." Liv also talked about how gender norms played significant roles in her processing of trauma sharing that she was feeling that she didn't want to fall into stereotypes of women as being overly sensitive or emotional.

Trauma Changes Everything

As I shared in the previous chapter, when I asked one of my participants, Aria, how they defined trauma, this is what they shared: "I think trauma is anything that happens to you or that you experience in your life that fundamentally changes, well honestly, everything." Aria's sentiment captures what many survivors of trauma encounter at some point in their journeys, which is that it's hard not to be impacted in some way and shaped by traumatic experiences, particularly those that lead to traumatization. As I will explore below, it's not that trauma inherently becomes the sole defining factor of how a person understands who they are. Yet, it's very difficult to put traumatic experiences aside once encountered in that they inform how survivors understand and make meaning of the world around them similarly to how any experiences or identities shape our perspectives.

What might this mean for college students who have experienced trauma? What is it like to be a college student navigating trauma? In the sections that follow, I explore those questions through the lens of four key domains where trauma has an impact for college students and shapes how they move through the world: (a) identity, (b) relationships, (c) environment, and (d) belonging.

Identity

For many college students, their time in higher education coincides with being in the developmental period of emerging adulthood, during which many questions about "Who am I?" are present. What happens, then, when you're trying to figure out your sense of who you are in the world while simultaneously navigating the ripple effects of traumatic experience? One of my participants, Beth, provided a beautiful metaphor of a sapling in a hurricane as a possible response to this question. Here is how she described what it's like to be someone who has experienced trauma while in college and how it impacted who she is in the world:

> you're in college . . . and you're still really forming who you are . . . and I think I am still forming who I am as a person, and so I think it's almost like—have you ever seen a tree that was hit by a hurricane when it was sapling? The tree bends, and it rights itself and grows back straight, but there's a little nick and bump in the tree. You look at it, and you're like, "Oh, it underwent something really nasty, but it kept going." I feel like

that's how I see myself.... I'm still the same person, I just have a little bump.... I don't let that bump keep me down. I'm still going to grow straight, I'm still growing, I'm still emerging and forming as a person.

What Beth described captures what I've learned over the years from many college students about their traumatic experiences. It's not that trauma becomes the sole way many students define themselves, but it is certainly present as an aspect of their identities and how they understand who they are in the world and in relation to others. This inevitably exists on a spectrum. Some students will feel more closely connected to defining themselves by their traumatic experiences than others, and this is likely to vary relative to distance from the trauma or in different contexts. For example, a student engaged in advocacy for survivors of sexual violence may feel more defined by their own traumatic experience of sexual violence while at an event to promote awareness or in a meeting with administrators who seem unwilling to understand the impact of policies and practices on survivors.

Something that has been particularly notable to me in my work about the intersection of trauma and college student identity development is that trauma can have the effect of creating additional developmental tasks for survivors to confront in their identity development (Shalka, 2019). For example, negotiating the tug and pull of changed relationships, navigating instances of forced disclosure, and making meaning of affective or embodied responses to trauma can all impact broader questions of "Who am I?" in the world. Sometimes responses to that question feel tentative and in flux for survivors of trauma as they make meaning of who they are in relation to the challenging circumstances they have endured.

Relationships

As is discussed in many places throughout this book, relationships are a critical component of recuperation from trauma (Shalka, 2022b; van der Kolk, 2014). Meanwhile, relationships are also a space of tremendous flux and tugs and pulls for those who have experienced trauma (Erikson, 1995; Shalka, 2019). On the one hand, trauma creates a need for survivors to have empathetic and supportive others that they can rely on through recovery. Yet, trauma can simultaneously create conditions that result in survivors needing to push others away. One of my research participants, Violet, shared the following in describing this tug-pull:

> There was definitely a dissonance there. I think I also became emotionally distant, but more intense where I would push people away but then I would desperately need them and not know how to articulate it. Sometimes I got upset and then I would get really emotional and really intense.

There are many reasons that relationships can be challenged or compromised in the context of trauma. One reason may be related to a survivor's sense of whether those around them understand what they're going through or not. One of my research participants, Liv, talked about this in terms of her experience feeling isolated and distant from her peers because they hadn't lived through something like she had in losing a close friend to suicide. Liv described this as "living out of the realm of [her friend group's] collective experience" and described it in the following way:

> [I had] my close friend group but, now, all of a sudden, I was the only one in that friend group who would have this experience and who is struggling with this, specifically at that time. That was really alienating, because I couldn't find that comfort in those relationships like I had been.

Some of the feelings that emerge in the aftermath of trauma are intense and may be challenging to hold in the context of relationships. Many students have shared with me the myriad ways they pull away from others as acts of protection. Whether it has been resident assistants who are careful to not release their emotions until they are away from their residents or previously extroverted students who just need to stay home alone and watch some Netflix, there are numerous examples of students who pull away from others after trauma. As one of my participants, Beth, shared with me, her fears and sense of vulnerability in the world were so intense after her father's suicide that she pulled away from others to protect herself, knowing that she couldn't share the intensity of those feelings with just anyone.

Sometimes, however, survivors equally have reasons to draw others nearer to them. Survivors need to be able to share their stories with others as mechanisms of healing. They need empathetic listeners who can sit with them and communicate, whether directly or indirectly, that the survivor is still a whole human worthy of being embraced and held in the social order. Empathetic relationships are where stability and rhythm and safety can be found again, all conditions that can be severely compromised because of trauma.

Meanwhile, trauma also has a way of helping to amplify our empathetic responses to others. Indeed, trauma can enhance a survivor's sense of interconnectedness and understanding with others. This sense of kinship with those who have experienced hardship and trauma is something I have heard repeatedly from participants in my research. Violet spoke of a spark that can happen between people when you've both experienced something traumatic as something that defies words and is instead a felt experience. She spoke of that instant as that "weird moment where both of your eyes lit up—'Oh, my God! You do that too!' . . . Sometimes you don't even realize how liberating that is until someone opens up."

Negotiations in the Environment

I have come to use the metaphor of a *shadow space* in talking about what it's like for survivors of trauma to navigate through campus environments (Shalka, 2021). That metaphor came while I was trying to think about what research participants had shared with me of their experiences moving through campus spaces. I was sitting in my dining room working through some of my data and glanced out the window as I let my mind wander about how to figure out the puzzle in front of me. I started thinking about how there are parts of my backyard that are fully lit by sunlight during some parts of the day and covered by shadows at other times when the sun moves and the trees provide some shade. The physical components of my yard are the same all day long—the trees and grass and shrubs are all there in light or shadow. But, despite the same physical parts, there's an embodied sense of difference when the shadows come. There's a visual difference of things looking a bit altered in the shadows, and there's even a felt sense of difference as the shadows often make the area feel cooler when I walk into it.

That reality of the physical parts all being the same in the shadows, but the *felt experience* being different captured what my participants were sharing with me. What I came to realize is that all the physical components of the campus were unchanged for students, but their experiences in relation to those people and things were sometimes very different than students around them who had perhaps not experienced similar kinds of trauma. Let me offer an example of how one of my participants, Jasmine, talked about how this shadow space could manifest. In this quote, Jasmine is describing what it was like for her walking around her campus the day after a triggering experience brought her back to her experience of being sexually assaulted:

> I was just in a daze. I just remember walking—like usually I'm a very connected person and I like seeing the people around me and smiling at the people around me and observing the people around me. . . . I like to see people and really, really see and observe people. I just didn't have that desire the next day and I just felt in a daze. It was just this foggy feeling, like a glaze was over me, and a glaze was over everyone else. . . . It felt like there were just clouds around me. I just didn't care, which is so out of character for me and I know myself well enough that when that happens to me, that I'm working through something. . . . I know I'm thinking through it and I'm processing it when I just block the physical space around me out.

In this quote, Jasmine articulates a sentiment shared by many of my participants, which is that the environment around them feels different because of trauma. It might feel different to them in reference to other points in their lives. It might even feel different compared with other students around them who haven't endured trauma.

Many of us move through various spaces in our day rather unconsciously, not thinking very much about them. Trauma, though, can make those same spaces that are so innocuous for others rather charged and salient with feelings of unsafety. Student survivors of trauma, then, may navigate campus environments through a lens of whether things are safe or unsafe (Shalka, 2021). This safety can be in terms of how survivors make calculations about whether they are going to be physically safe in certain environments, but it also manifests in terms of how survivors consider spaces in terms of their safety to self and integrity.

Let me share a poignant example to illustrate these types of navigations. In the introduction of this book, I opened with the experience of one of my participants, Amira, who experienced both pervasive (such as discrimination and body shaming) and event-based (including having her hijab ripped off her head while walking to her car one evening) forms of trauma. Collectively, these experiences meant that Amira navigated the campus environment with a keen eye on what was safe or potentially unsafe.

One way that this manifested was that Amira was critically aware of where walls were as a potential source of safety. Amira's legitimate concern of having her hijab ripped off again meant that she fervently avoided situations where someone could get behind her and have that opportunity again. Thus, Amira tried to arrive early to classes to get a seat with her back against a wall. If she couldn't get there in time, she had a choice to make—whether she would try to negotiate with classmates to switch seats with her. I could easily imagine how awkward or anxiety-provoking that could be in various situations. Some days, Amira did ultimately decide that negotiation was too much for her, and she would then just not attend class. The environment felt too unsafe to support the very reason Amira was presumably in college—to be a student.

Some of my participants spoke of the felt "exhaustion" of these kinds of navigations in their campus environments. In so many ways, campus environments and interactions aren't built with the safety and recuperation of survivors of trauma in mind. For some participants in my research, the exhaustion came from the constant reality of moving through the campus in terms of bracing for the "what if?" *What if someone pulls off my hijab again? What if I see the man who sexually assaulted me somewhere on campus?* For others, the campus environment was exhausting because there were so many places and spaces that felt unsafe or triggering. A classroom space may be made unsafe by a professor who shows a video with triggering material without warning. A campus party may be made unsafe by the density of people there that remind a survivor of sexual assault of feelings and impressions associated with her own experience of assault. In short, campus environments provide no shortage of examples of situations, interactions, and spaces that can feel unsafe and/or triggering, and that takes a toll—there is a tremendous physical, psychic, and spiritual energy that goes into these kinds of negotiations and maneuvers for survivors.

Belonging and Community

A sense of belonging is a dimension of students' experiences that we increasingly pay attention to in student affairs practice. In part, a sense of belonging has emerged on the radar as important to foster because it's connected to many important student outcomes of higher education including persistence and academic performance (Strayhorn, 2019). Belonging represents the degree to which students feel supported, accepted, connected, and that they matter to others in the context of their college communities—to the extent students feel this kind of integration within a campus community, they're more likely to be able to achieve many of the important milestones of higher education.

Sadly, though, I've learned in my own research how complicated a sense of belonging can be for students who have experienced trauma. In a study I did with Christina Leal (Shalka & Leal, 2022), we learned that undergraduate students who identified as having PTSD experienced a diminished sense of belonging relative to their peers who did not have PTSD. As we explored this finding further, we learned that a sense of belonging for students with PTSD was significantly impacted relative to students' sense of safety on their campuses, perceptions that those seeking mental health treatment would be viewed negatively, and perceptions of a more negative campus climate in terms of mental health.

In some of my qualitative research, I've learned more about the tremendous complexity of a sense of belonging after trauma. On the one hand, participants have explained the ways they feel isolated and alienated in their campus communities after trauma. Sometimes that was strongly connected to not being validated in their trauma whether that was because others didn't know about their experiences or if they did know did not acknowledge those experiences as trauma. This reminded me every time I heard such examples as to why it's so important we embrace inclusive definitions of trauma and leave space for those who have experienced trauma to self-identify.

Another complicated element of belonging that I observed in my research was rather heartbreaking to me. Many students experiencing trauma felt their peers wouldn't understand. Survivors had to develop strategies to stay connected to peers in light of this reality, but it sometimes came at a cost, especially when the strategy endorsed was silence. Survivors would find ways to just not talk with their peers about what was going on for them as a mechanism to remain connected and in community. While remaining silent about their authentic experiences of trauma allowed student survivors to stay connected in peer groups on the one hand, it also came at the price of authenticity in relationships. Paige very poignantly explained this in the following way:

> I think one of the strongest feelings was really just loneliness and separation and feeling like, when I wasn't saying anything, I lost a sense of belonging because people didn't know the real me. But then, again, that fear that if I did voice things, I would lose a sense of belonging if people didn't validate me.

Meanwhile, my research participants have also helped me understand the ways in which belonging can be enhanced for them when they're surrounded by people in their campus communities who meet them with care and compassion. One of my participants, April, reached a point after her mother's murder of acknowledging that her world was not ok. Yet, in the context of her campus community where she felt so well supported, she could find that small sense of being ok. She called her campus "home" in a way that spoke to the belonging she felt there. It also spoke to all the supportive people in April's campus community who helped bring moments of ease to her when her life was otherwise filled with anything but. That is the positive piece, and is so incredibly encouraging to me, because that's something we can tangibly do something about in higher education. We can be active in relationship-building and equity work to ensure students are surrounded by care, compassion, and accurate empathy and understanding; that is, the proactive work we need to engage in as we work toward a more trauma-informed practice that is entirely within our reach.

Conclusion

There's often a lot more going on for students who have experienced trauma than we may see or know on the surface. A large part of our work in student affairs related to student trauma is enhancing our own capacities to better see and understand what that impact may be and ultimately to believe student survivors of trauma when they share with us what they have experienced and how they feel in the world as a result. As we begin discussing more specific orientations to trauma-informed practice in the coming chapters, the most fundamental work remains that of learning to attune ourselves to considering "What else might be going on?" for those with whom we interact. Creating this space for possibilities beyond what is immediately visible to us opens up potentialities of care and humanity toward recuperation.

References

Arnett, J. J. (2006). Emerging adulthood: Understanding a new way of coming of age. In J. J. Arnett & J. L. Tanner (Eds), *Emerging adults in America: Coming of age in the 21st century* (pp. 3–19). American Psychological Association.

Arnett, J. J. (2015). Introduction: Emerging adulthood theory and research: Where we are and where we should go. In J. J. Arnett (Ed.), *The Oxford handbook of emerging adulthood* (pp. 1–7). Oxford University Press.

Baxter Magolda, M. B. (2009). *Authoring your life: Developing an internal voice to navigate life's challenges*. Stylus.

Blimling, G. S. (2013). New dimensions to psychosocial development in traditionally aged college students. *About Campus*, 5(18), 10–16. https://doi.org/10.1002/abc.21132

Breslau, N. (2009). The epidemiology of trauma, PTSD, and other posttrauma disorders. *Trauma, Violence, & Abuse*, 10(3), 198–210. https://doi.org/10.1177/1524838009334448

Brison S. J. (2002). *Aftermath: Violence and the remaking of a self*. Princeton University Press.

Brown, L. S. (2008). *Cultural competence in trauma therapy: Beyond the flashback.* American Psychological Association.

Comas-Días, L., Hall, G. N., & Neville, H. A. (2019). Racial trauma: Theory, research, and healing: Introduction to the special issue. *American Psychologist, 74*(1), 1–5. https://dx.doi.org/10.1037/amp0000442

Erikson, K. (1995). Notes on trauma and community. In C. Caruth (Ed.), *Trauma: Explorations in memory* (pp. 183–199). Johns Hopkins University Press.

Felitti, V. J., Anda, R. F., Nordenberg, D., Williamson, D. F., Spitz, A. M., Edwards, V., Koss, M. P., & Marks, J. S. (1998). Relationship of childhood abuse and household dysfunction to many of the leading causes of death in adults: The adverse childhood experiences (ACE) study. *American Journal of Preventative Medicine, 14*(4), 245–258.

Herman, J. L. (2015). *Trauma and recovery: The aftermath of violence—from domestic abuse to political terror.* Basic Books.

Hernández-Wolfe, P. (2013). *A borderlands view on Latinos, Latin Americans, and decolonization: Rethinking mental health.* Aronson.

Johnson, A. G. (2014). *The gender knot: Unraveling our patriarchal legacy* (3rd ed.). Temple University Press.

Kilmer, R. P. (2014). Resilience and posttraumatic growth in children. In L. G. Calhoun & R. G. Tedeschi (Eds.), *Handbook of posttraumatic growth: Research and practice* (pp. 264–288). Routledge.

Okello, W. K., & Shalka, T. R. (2022). Introduction to trauma-informed practice in student affairs. In T. R. Shalka & W. K. Okello (Eds.), *Trauma-informed practice in student affairs: Multidimensional considerations for care, healing, and wellbeing* (New Directions for Student Services, Vol. 177, pp. 7–15). Wiley. https://doi.org/10.1002/ss.20410

Oprah Daily. (2021, December 1). *Brené Brown explains why we need to rethink "walking in someone else's shoes"* [Video]. Facebook. https://www.facebook.com/oprahdaily/videos/brené-brown-explains-why-we-need-to-rethink-walking-in-someone-elses-shoes/2966387070247664/

Perry, B. D., & Winfrey, O. (2021). *What happened to you? Conversations on trauma, resilience, and healing.* Flatiron Books.

Perry, W. G., Jr. (1968). *Forms of intellectual and ethical development in the college years: A scheme.* President and Fellows of Harvard College.

Read, J. P., Ouimette, P., White, J., Colder, C., & Farrow, S. (2011). Rates of *DSM-IV-TR* trauma exposure and posttraumatic stress disorder among newly matriculated college students. *Psychological Trauma: Theory, Research, Practice, and Policy, 3*(2), 148–156. https://doi.org/10.1037/a0021260

Shalka, T. R. (2019). Trauma and the interpersonal landscape: Developmental tasks of the relational self identity site. *Journal of College Student Development, 60*(1), 35–51. https://doi.org/10.1353/csd.2019.0002

Shalka, T. R. (2021). Traversing the shadow space: Experiences of spatiality after college student trauma. *The Review of Higher Education, 45*(1), 93–116. https://doi.org/10.1353/rhe.0.0176

Shalka, T. R. (2022a). How a trauma-informed organization would change the face of higher education (and why we need it now more than ever). *Change: The Magazine of Higher Learning, 54*(4), 4–10. https://doi.org/10.1080/00091383.2022.2078148

Shalka, T. R. (2022b). Nurturing a trauma-informed student affairs division. *About Campus, 27*(2), 18–25. https://doi.org/10.1177/10864822221100253

Shalka, T. R., & Leal, C. C. (2022). Sense of belonging for college students with PTSD: The role of safety, stigma, and campus climate. *Journal of American College Health, 70*(3), 698–705. https://doi.org/10.1080/07448481.2020.1762608

Strayhorn, T. L. (2019). *College students' sense of belonging: A key to educational success for all students* (2nd ed.). Routledge.

U.S. Department of Education, National Center for Education Statistics. (2020). Table 303.50: Total fall enrollment in degree-granting postsecondary institutions, by level of enrollment, control and level of institution, attendance status, and age of student: 2019. In *Digest of education statistics* (2020 ed.). U.S. Department of Education, National Center for Education Statistics.

van der Kolk, B. A. (2014). *The body keeps the score: Brain, mind, and body in the healing of trauma*. Viking.

Venet, A. S. (2021). *Equity-centered trauma-informed education*. W. W. Norton & Company.

3
What Does It Mean to Be Trauma-Informed?

Kimberlé Crenshaw is a renowned legal scholar, perhaps best known for developing the concept of intersectionality. Intersectionality is a framework that draws our attention to how interlocks of systems of oppression (such as racism and sexism) produce unique realities that can't be explained fully by looking at discrete systems of race or gender alone (Crenshaw, 1989, 1991). In Crenshaw's (1989) original work around the concept, she illustrated intersectionality in terms of how the legal system had been able to account for sexism and racism discretely, but not simultaneously as a unique system of discrimination for Black women in the workplace. The power of a concept like intersectionality is that it provides a framework to identify and articulate a specific phenomenon that is otherwise unseen by particular systems. As Crenshaw has explained, "When facts don't fit the frame, people can't hold them" (Rivas, 2020, para. 15). In other words, sometimes there are things we can't quite understand until presented with some basic tools by which to approach and hold the facts that are being presented to us.

The importance of the frame is a powerful metaphor in terms of intersectionality and legal systems, to be sure, and I also find it to be a poignant metaphor for the work we do in trauma-informed systems. I am drawing on Crenshaw's thinking here for a couple of reasons related to trauma-informed practice in student affairs. First, without trauma-informed work, it's entirely possible that our organizations can proceed from a stance of trauma and adversity neutrality. This neutrality stance creates invisibility of traumatic experiences among members of our communities at best, and further harm, re-traumatization or new traumatization at worst. Second, connecting this chapter to Crenshaw's work also highlights a critical need in trauma-informed practice, which is that it must be power-conscious. In many ways that have been illustrated in previous chapters, trauma and systemic oppression travel in parallel and often intersecting pathways. When we're talking about trauma work, we're also talking about equity work in a variety of ways. In essence, what we're trying to do in building trauma-informed systems is to create a "frame" to guide our practice and hold space for safety and recuperation for all members of a community. In this chapter, I will provide an overview of what we might mean when we say "trauma-informed" and offer an initial framework to work with in embracing a trauma-informed practice in student affairs.

Why Is Trauma-Informed Practice Important in Higher Education?

Our peers on the K-12 side of the educational landscape are slightly ahead of our curve in higher education in terms of taking notice of trauma in their communities. If you do a Google search about trauma-informed practice in schools, you will get a robust list of results about the work happening in K-12 settings to create trauma-informed conditions supportive of both student and educator success. Meanwhile, trauma-informed practice in higher education is a more nascent topic.

What brought us to this point of paying attention to trauma-informed practice in higher education? A constellation of factors. One significant catalyst occurred with the Obama administration's White House Task Force to Protect Students from Sexual Assault (2017) that in its first report highlighted the need to train campus officials on trauma-informed practice. Sexual violence, however, is just one of many factors that have amplified awareness in higher education about trauma in the lives of students. For example, an increase in student veterans in higher education after wars in Iraq and Afghanistan renewed both public and campus awareness of the possibility of PTSD. Following the murder of George Floyd and countless other Black lives at the hands of police, there has also been a growing awareness on many campuses that racism can be experienced as traumatic. Continued gun violence and campus shootings make us aware all too often of the need for support after trauma that impacts entire campus communities. Finally, the global COVID-19 pandemic has contributed to many campus officials recognizing the possibility of trauma being present among students, faculty, and staff and the need to approach our work through the lens of trauma-informed practice.

There are many compelling reasons to pay attention to trauma in the lives of college students. We know from research that trauma can place strains on students' capacities to be successful in educational environments. For example, trauma has been correlated with negative impacts on students' academic achievement, persistence, and even a sense of belonging (Boyraz et al., 2013, 2016; Shalka & Leal, 2022). When students face negative ripple effects of trauma and are triggered into states of either hyperarousal or hypoarousal, their capacities to learn and engage with others can be compromised (van der Kolk, 2014). In short, many of the goals we have for students during their time in higher education can be impacted by traumatic experiences.

Although trauma-informed practice doesn't erase trauma from the lives of students, it does contribute to minimizing trauma's negative impact in educational environments in two important ways. First, trauma-informed practice provides needed support to those who have been impacted by trauma. Second, trauma-informed practice allows us to avoid re-traumatization and/or creating new traumas for students. Let's dig into this further below.

What Is a Trauma-Informed Practice?

Trauma-informed practice is increasingly a buzzword in many different communities of practice, but what exactly does it mean to evoke this term? Simply put, trauma-informed practice in higher education is about taking knowledge about trauma to directly inform and shape our policies and practices (Pope, 2022). Trauma-informed practice is a response to the reality that many individuals are impacted by trauma and have experienced potentially traumatic experiences in their lives. A trauma-informed practice, then, represents an approach that members of a particular organization can adopt in creating spaces and interactions that can help to nurture relationships, safety, predictability, and care (Okello & Shalka, 2022; SAMHSA, 2014; Venet, 2021). We can think of trauma-informed work as having two primary explicit goals: (1) supporting those who have been impacted by trauma and (2) working to not create additional trauma or re-traumatization (Venet, 2021). These approaches must be attentive to both individual- and systems-level needs and efforts. Trauma-informed practice is proactive as much as it is reactive (Okello & Shalka, 2022).

Sometimes it's helpful to see what something isn't to fully understand what it is, so let me offer an example of a situation that was clearly missing a trauma-informed approach. Mia, one of my research participants, experienced a traumatic event shortly before the semester started. She and her mom were at a gas station on their way home one night, when some men pulled them both out of their car and proceeded to physically assault Mia's mom as Mia watched helplessly. Flash forward a little over a month later and Mia was in a class that had a project due that day. Based on Mia's accounts of the classroom experience, it was clear to me that the professor had created an environment that was stressful and toxic. All of that was independent of Mia's experience of trauma, and the professor didn't know what Mia had suffered. That said, the way the professor led the class created a perfect storm for Mia the day that project was due. Mia got completely overwhelmed and ultimately had a panic attack in the middle of class. The professor seemed ill-equipped to navigate what was happening to Mia. In fact, it took another student in the class to name that Mia was having a panic attack and to coordinate getting Mia help. In Mia's next interaction with the professor, the professor seemed to continue to be ill-equipped in their response. Rather than recognizing that something else might be going on, the professor seemed convinced Mia's reaction was about her project and the professor assured Mia that they could fix the project. Mia summarized that the professor failed to "get it."

In Mia's example, the two explicit goals of trauma-informed practice (supporting those impacted by trauma and working to not create additional trauma) were clearly not met. Mia wasn't supported. The professor's approach and toxic classroom environment meant not only that Mia didn't feel supported by the professor or in that space, but simultaneously that Mia was further harmed. When I think about

Mia's example, it's not that I expect the professor to have waved a magic wand to make Mia's suffering go away. Nor do I expect that the professor should have been a mind reader to know about Mia's trauma. Frankly, we never need to know the specifics of a student's trauma to create conditions for recuperation. What I do want, however, are faculty and administrators who lean on principles of trauma-informed practice to guide their work. Had that been the case in Mia's example, it would have meant a more supportive, relational, and predictable experience that at the very least wouldn't have created further harm.

One common concern about trauma-informed practice in educational environments is whether this is really the work of administrators and faculty. Sometimes people hear "trauma-informed" and push back with, "Wait! I'm not a therapist. I'm not qualified to do this kind of work." This is a really important point to clarify. Trauma-informed practice is not intended to function as an alternative to or replacement for therapy or other healing modalities that survivors may engage in their processes of recuperation. Critically, we're not asking members of our communities to work as clinicians when that isn't what they're trained to do. Instead, we're asking members of our community to engage in trauma-informed work by (a) recognizing that trauma is prevalent in our communities, (b) seeking to gain knowledge about how trauma impacts members of our community, and (c) working toward creating practices, policies, and interactions that create conditions for recuperation and reduce further harm or re-traumatization (Okello & Shalka, 2022; SAMHSA, 2014; Venet, 2021).

I shared the example of Mia to illustrate a situation that certainly lacked a trauma-informed lens. I'd like to offer a counterpoint to that illustration from another one of my research participants, April, who was supported in all the right ways imaginable by her campus community. During April's junior year of college, she received the horrific news that her mom had been murdered. April characterized that day as the day she "lost [her] whole world." Simultaneously, she had nothing but good things to say about the administrators and faculty on her campus and the ways they helped her through this indescribable tragedy. She spoke of administrators by saying that "they really helped me out after this whole situation. They took everything into their hands and completely took a weight off my shoulder."

Whether the administrators and faculty April was interacting with had training about trauma or not, they were clearly operating in ways that were congruent with trauma-informed practice. The school learned about what happened before April did—an administrator met April after class and took her to a safe and private office location where a counselor and the head of campus police were waiting. Together, they called the police office in April's town, where an officer communicated to her what had happened. The news was devastating, of course, yet these administrators had done the best they could to support April as she received that news by bringing her to a safe and private place and ensuring there were people there who could help her, including her boyfriend. In the weeks and months that followed, April had story after story of campus administrators trying to make things easier for her as she dealt with layer upon layer of working through the aftermath of tragedy. When April was worried about how to afford college without financial support from her family, administrators stepped in and figured it all out with the financial aid office for her. When April acquired her family dogs to care for (which would have been a problem with housing policies), the housing office coordinated getting an on-campus apartment for April and her boyfriend to move into along with the dogs and said not to worry about the dog policy. April also had frequent visits from some of the upper-level administrators on her campus, and by the time we were talking she told me that she had very close relationships with some of them. Administrators coordinated with all of April's faculty and worked out plans for what she would need once she returned to campus and resumed classes, and continued to do this on her behalf any time she needed to be away, something she described as alleviating a lot of stress.

There are so many examples in April's story of what it means to do trauma-informed work. There was attention to April's sense of safety and control throughout. There were moments of humanizing as the driving force of decisions over restrictive policies that could have caused more damage. Fundamentally, there was attentiveness to wrapping April with a network of supportive people who were interested in building authentic relationships with her. It was clear throughout my time with April that her institution's response wasn't just one of dealing with an immediate crisis—it was a response of seeing a fellow human in pain and working to ease their burden wherever possible. April shared her assessment that her institution "does a really good job with traumas." I agreed with her evaluation. Many of the elements that were undergirding her institution's responses will be reflected in some of the trauma-informed practice frameworks that I share below.

A Few Models of Trauma-Informed Practice

As mentioned earlier, approaches to trauma-informed practice in higher education are still in their infancy relative to some other domains. Given that, understanding approaches to trauma-informed practice that are used and working in other contexts is a useful place to start in imagining what trauma-informed approaches could look like in higher education. Below, I offer some strong examples of models of trauma-informed practice that provide some excellent ideas to think with in moving toward a trauma-informed practice that is higher education situated.

A frequently leaned-on approach to trauma-informed practice comes from the Substance Abuse and Mental Health Services Administration (SAMHSA, 2014). SAMHSA begins with several key assumptions about work in a trauma-informed system that they characterize in terms of four "Rs": (1) We need to begin by *realizing* the prevalence and impact of trauma; (2) we then have to *recognize* how trauma may manifest in terms of signs and symptoms of individuals and systems; (3) then, we're able to *respond* by incorporating trauma-informed practices into our work; and (4) finally, we must be cognizant of and actively seek to resist practices that lead to *re-traumatization*. Collectively, these assumptions offer an important mindset in terms of how we need to approach our work.

Following these assumptions, SAMHSA (2014) then outlines six principles of trauma-informed work which include the following: (a) safety (i.e., working to ensure members of an organization feel both psychological and physical safety); (b) trustworthiness and transparency (i.e., organizational processes and decisions are transparent to help foster trust); (c) peer support (i.e., mechanisms are established for peer support and mutual self-help); (d) collaboration and mutuality (i.e., a recognition that everyone has a role to play in trauma-informed work); (e) empowerment, voice, and choice (i.e., power is often compromised by trauma, so trauma-informed practice emphasizes resilience, empowerment, and choice); and (f) cultural, historical, and gender issues (i.e., addressing the needs that arise in the context of systems of power and privilege).

A recent and powerful approach to trauma-informed practice in education is that of Alex Shevrin Venet's (2021) *Equity-Centered Trauma-Informed Education*. I appreciate many things about Venet's work including the holistic approach presented and the starting point that trauma and social justice are inextricably connected. Although primarily situated in K-12 settings, the ideas and principles that Venet advances are easily applicable and translatable to higher education. Let me begin by naming two key points about the intersection of trauma and equity that Venet shares which are that "inequity causes trauma" and "school isn't equitable for trauma-affected students" (p. xix). These are important starting points in thinking about the work we have to do in educational systems related to trauma-informed practice. As I mentioned previously, trauma-informed practice is equity work.

Venet's (2021) model of equity-centered trauma-informed education is grounded in six principles:

1. Our trauma-informed work must be antiracist and anti-oppression.
2. We ground our practice in asset-based rather than deficit-based approaches with particular attention to the reality that "trauma is a normal response to threat" (p. 13).
3. Trauma-informed work is systems oriented.
4. We maintain a human-centered approach.
5. Trauma-informed education is conceived as universal and proactive.
6. Trauma-informed practice is explicitly focused on social justice.

From these principles, Venet (2021) offers four critical shifts to embrace toward equity-centered trauma-informed practice. First, we must shift from being reactionary in addressing the needs of those who have been traumatized, to also pay attention to the proactive work that needs to happen in a trauma-informed system (Shift 1:

from reactive to proactive). Second, we must engage in approaching others with unconditional positive regard as opposed to broken and in need of rescue (Shift 2: from a savior mentality to unconditional positive regard focused on others' skills and values). Third, we need to shift from thinking of trauma-informed work as the responsibility of just a few individuals and instead embrace it as the work of an entire system (Shift 3: from the responsibility of a few to embedded in policies and practices of an entire system). Finally, we need to shift from seeing the impacts of trauma at a local level to understanding the potential of our trauma-informed practices having broader reach (Shift 4: from focusing on how trauma impacts particular educational spaces to seeing how we can use trauma-informed practices as a change toward equity and justice broadly).

Advancing a Model of Trauma-Informed Practice in Student Affairs

We now have a lot of information about what might be useful in building our frame for a trauma-informed student affairs practice. But what would trauma-informed practice more specifically look like in student affairs practice? What do we need to pay attention to and embrace to fully approach our work through this lens? In this section, I offer some translations. In other words, I'm distilling the literature and research about trauma and trauma-informed practice to situate this work more specifically in a student affairs context.

Let me begin by offering six guideposts for us to work with. These guideposts undergird any work we do in a trauma-informed student affairs practice whether at the individual or systemic levels. I propose that trauma-informed practice in student affairs should be:

1. Holistic
2. Power-conscious and anti-oppression
3. Focused on relationships
4. Committed to knowledge-building
5. Harm reducing
6. Committed to wellness-centered decision-making and practice

What Does It Mean to Be Holistic?

Trauma is often both understood and communicated about in terms of the individual or sometimes a particular community that has been impacted. Although there are many instances of an individual or community being primarily impacted by trauma, traumatic experiences inevitably don't stay contained at these levels. As shared in Chapter 1, trauma has a way of rippling beyond the individual into relationships, communities, and across generations.

A holistic approach to trauma-informed practice recognizes that many individuals are directly impacted by trauma and many others are impacted indirectly. It also recognizes that our work is not simply about reactive responses to trauma, but simultaneously proactive efforts. Holistic approaches maintain broad conceptualizations of trauma to make sure we're attentive to traumatic experiences in their varied forms, while recognizing the reality that restrictive definitions often exclude along boundaries already divided by oppression and minoritization. Additionally, as Venet (2021) reminds us "we must make sure we see trauma as a structural issue, not just an individual one" (p. 8). We must look structurally and culturally in understanding the ways in which particular contexts and systems are part of the problem. That involves work to excavate our practices deeply, as opposed to just viewing trauma-informed work as offering resources to those primarily impacted by trauma.

What Does It Mean to Be Power-Conscious and Anti-Oppression?

Trauma always exists in the context of power and oppression. Sometimes that means oppressive systems are the sources of trauma, which is certainly the case in experiences such as racial trauma and gender-based violence. Sometimes oppressive systems create further harm and challenge survivors' capacities to move through trauma. This can be the case, for example, when gender norms restrict someone's ability to authentically share what they are experiencing for fear of being seen as weak (Shalka, 2019a).

Ultimately, trauma and oppression are connected in complicated ways. If we're doing the work of helping communities to heal from and minimize trauma, we must simultaneously be doing the explicit work of anti-racism and anti-oppression in all of its forms. Thus, a trauma-informed system must be attentive to dimensions such as campus climate, micro and macro experiences of safety or lack thereof, and actively working to dismantle systems and practices of oppression in our campus communities.

What Does It Mean to Be Focused on Relationships?

Relationships are critical in recuperation from trauma. There's no way to overemphasize that point. There is a large and broad body of research that demonstrates this point repeatedly (e.g., Erikson, 1995; Shalka, 2019b; van der Kolk, 2014). Knowing that, a key priority in any trauma-informed practice must be that of intentional work to building and strengthening authentic relationships that uphold an ethos of care and humanity in a community.

What students, faculty, and staff will need on the other side of trauma are empathetic others. This seems straightforward enough, but the problem is that it's better when those relationships are already present rather than trying to establish them after the fact. I've talked to too many students over the years who never knew who to go to on their campuses after trauma and they suffered the effects of isolation as a result. It is thus imperative that a trauma-informed student affairs practice is fundamentally grounded in paying attention to ensuring all students on our campuses are connected to faculty and staff in meaningful ways so they have someone to go to when needed. It's also imperative that we're attentive to building supportive and quality relationships for staff and faculty so that they have support and a sense of worth in their communities. This contributes to harm reduction but also ensures staff and faculty are well supported when they are exposed to students' traumas secondarily or confronting their own trauma.

What Does It Mean to Be Committed to Knowledge Building?

One of the basic components of a trauma-informed system is recognizing that trauma is prevalent among members of the community (SAMHSA, 2014), but recognition only gets us so far. We must then take that recognition and do something about it. The logical next step is to build the collective capacity of members of a community to not only know that trauma is present but also recognize the impacts of trauma and how it may travel through communities.

A sometimes-overlooked component of traumatic experience is isolation. One factor that contributes to feelings of isolation is when survivors of trauma don't feel that others understand what they're going through (Shalka, 2019b). An antidote to this challenge is education. We need to commit to having members of our student affairs communities build collective knowledge around what trauma is, how those who endure trauma may react, and how trauma impacts our organizations.

What Does It Mean to Be Harm Reducing?

Trauma-informed practice is not simply about reacting to trauma and supporting those impacted. It's also about being mindful and intentional to not create further harm. In organizations of all kinds, including colleges and universities, we sometimes (often unintentionally I would like to believe) re-traumatize individuals who have experienced trauma while in other cases our actions and policies actually create trauma (Shalka, 2022).

When we're oriented to harm reduction, we are actively scanning our policies and practices for the possibility of re-traumatization or creating trauma so that we can prevent either scenario. Our practice becomes grounded in creating safety, choice, and empowerment (SAMHSA, 2014). Our practice is rooted in compassion and care while at the same time power-conscious in recognizing the ways that systems of oppression coded into our organizational practices and interactions can function as uninterrogated sources of harm (Venet, 2021).

What Does It Mean to Be Committed to Wellness-Centered Decision-Making and Practice?

Our trauma-informed work is fundamentally about creating cultures of care (Shalka, 2022). This orientation allows us to focus on wholeness and humanity as we work toward systems that support wellness. By wellness, I don't mean pushing self-care onto individuals and/or offering a massage therapist chair for an afternoon to staff. Yes, there is plenty everyone in a community can and should do to engage in their own self-care *and* that is not where it can end. Wellness cannot be pushed solely onto individuals—it must be structurally supported at the level of organizations.

Wellness-centered decision-making and practice are committed to caring for helpers—the staff, faculty, and students who are supporting others. It is about attention to the potential for secondary traumatic stress and/or burnout among staff. It is about creating work conditions in which staff can thrive in terms of engaging meaningfully while not being overwhelmed by unrealistic expectations or insufficient resources to fulfill their roles. It is about normalizing balance rather than valorizing and upholding long work weeks, 24/7 availability, or the like as metrics of success. In 2021, Portugal passed a law that makes it illegal for supervisors to email or text employees after work hours about work-related business (Horowitz & Cotovio, 2021)—isn't that some interesting food for thought?

How Do We Put This Into Practice?

It can feel daunting to imagine where to begin with trauma-informed practice and the guideposts above because there is frankly a lot of work to do in higher education on this front. That said, the place to start is exactly where we are. We start with what we can do, and we do that work intentionally.

I sometimes hear subtle and overt pushback to why student affairs professionals feel like they can't do trauma-informed work. One popular one is, "But I'm not a counselor." Another is, "But I'm not a supervisor" or "I'm not leading a unit/division. Doesn't this have to come from the top?" A final pushback is, "I'm already overworked and have so much on my plate. I don't have time for another latest fad."

I do have some specific responses to each of those concerns, but the details are likely not as important as my overall message that trauma-informed practice isn't about adding new things on as much as it is developing particular lenses and ways of being so that all of our work begins to flow from that starting point. The ways we ultimately put this work into practice is by embracing our organizational positionality. No matter where we're situated in the hierarchies and organizational charts, we begin in our sphere of influence. We learn about trauma and we begin to consider and then operationalize the things in our immediate practice that we can do through a trauma-informed lens. Maybe that comes through how we write a particular policy, how we interact with our colleagues, or the kinds of questions we ask ourselves. Maybe that comes in the way we plan a program, challenge the status quo, prepare a room, or demand space to breathe. We begin this work where we are and through and with the people and practices we touch.

Thinking Individually and Systemically

I was in a meeting a while ago that was an example of something many of us who work in higher education in any capacity have probably seen unfold at some point in our careers—what was happening in the meeting had absolutely nothing to do with the named topic of the discussion. On the one hand, I had colleagues who organized a process for working through the task at hand. On the other hand, many people in the group were experiencing confusion about the process and what was being asked of everyone. In the middle of this work to clarify a process is where the example of the meeting not being about the meeting started. It was clear as the conversation progressed that there was a lot of distrust and frustration in the group that had been fostered over many years of complex interactions and circumstances.

The focal point of the meeting erupted when one colleague grew increasingly frustrated and began to vocalize that. Their frustration was palpable, and it created an opening that other colleagues began to jump into and share some similar frustrations or different interpretations of what wasn't working that day at the meeting. In the meantime, the colleagues who had organized the process were left watching their plan derailed, yet admitted that they hadn't provided the group with the information they needed to proceed with the task. The conversation continued to get increasingly heated and the original colleague who had expressed frustrations had clearly had enough and left.

In the hours, days, and weeks following that meeting, I was intrigued to learn all the interpretations of what had happened that day. Some colleagues were scolding those who had expressed frustration for being disrespectful to their colleagues who had organized the process. Some people expressed to me that they found the whole scene incredibly painful and difficult to watch, especially because it had gotten so emotionally heated. Others expressed to me that they were grateful for the colleague who introduced the frustration because they felt the same way but hadn't felt there was space to express their opinions without that opening created. What was most fascinating to me was that some clear camps emerged. One camp clearly thought the problem was with the colleague who expressed the original frustration and that their behavior was out of line. The other camp saw that colleague as stating a truth that needed to be articulated.

My own interpretation of the event is likely informed by the trauma lens that I carry with me—I did understand how others were harmed by the way the colleague expressed their frustration *and* I did not see the reaction as something that should be interpreted as solely a problem of the individual. Instead, I recognized that nobody reacts in a meeting that way without more to the story. And the more to the story that I interpreted was that the organization itself had produced sufficient harm over time. Thus, while the individual was considering how they had impacted others the organization also needed to take responsibility for its role in why and how a colleague could get to that point in a meeting.

That *both/and* is what I want to discuss further in this section. It is tempting and easy to view trauma as a "problem" of the individual, but we also need to view an individual in the context of a system. We need to commit to thinking about trauma both individually *and* systemically, in terms of both its roots and ripples. As I begin to move forward in subsequent chapters about how to embrace trauma-informed practice in student affairs, try to hold onto that both/and as well as the many other points of complexity and beautiful messiness this work demands of us. We're being called to live in the ambiguity and liminality through trauma, and while that space is at times distressing and uncomfortable, it is also a space of rich potentialities and new ways of being.

Conclusion

This chapter articulated more explicitly what it means to do trauma-informed work in student affairs. I offered six key guideposts to undergird our trauma-informed practice in student affairs including that it should be: holistic; power-conscious and anti-oppression; focused on relationships; committed to knowledge-building; harm-reducing; and committed to wellness-centered decision-making and practice. These concepts help to provide a frame to move forward with in shaping what this work might look like in practice. In the chapters that follow, we will begin to encounter trauma-informed practice in much more tangible terms looking at our individual practices, our work directly with student survivors and student leaders, and finally through the lens of our organizations and campus systems.

References

Boyraz, G., Granda, R., Baker, C. N., Tidwell, L. L., & Waits, J. B. (2016). Posttraumatic stress, effort regulation, and academic outcomes among college students: A longitudinal study. *Journal of Counseling Psychology, 63*(4), 475–486. https://doi.org/10.1037/cou0000102

Boyraz, G., Horne, S. G., Owens, A. C., & Armstrong, A. P. (2013). Academic achievement and college persistence of African American students with trauma exposure. *Journal of Counseling Psychology, 60*, 582–592. https://doi.org/10.1037/a0033672

Crenshaw, K. (1989). Demarginalizing the intersection of race and sex: A Black feminist critique of antidiscrimination doctrine, feminist theory and antiracist politics. *University of Chicago Legal Forum, 1989*, 139–167.

Crenshaw, K. (1991). Mapping the margins: Intersectionality, identity politics, and violence against women of color. *Stanford Law Review, 43*(6), 1241–1299.

Erikson, K. (1995). Notes on trauma and community. In C. Caruth (Ed.), *Trauma: Explorations in memory* (pp. 183–199). Johns Hopkins University Press.

Horowitz, J., & Cotovio, V. (2021, November 11). In Portugal, it's now illegal for your boss to call outside work hours. *CNN.* https://www.cnn.com/2021/11/11/success/portugal-employer-contact-law/index.html

Okello, W. K., & Shalka, T. R. (2022). Introduction to trauma-informed practice in student affairs. In T. R. Shalka & W. K. Okello (Eds.), *Trauma-informed practice in student affairs: Multidimensional considerations for care, healing, and wellbeing* (New Directions for Student Services, Vol. 177, pp. 7–15). Wiley. https://doi.org/10.1002/ss.20410

Pope, R. (Host). (2022, May 11). Trauma-informed practice. *Student Affairs NOW* [Audio podcast episode No. 97]. https://studentaffairsnow.com/trauma-informed/

Rivas, M. (2020, July 9). Understanding intersectionality is crucial to our current progress. *Shondaland.* https://www.shondaland.com/act/news-politics/a33028611/understanding-intersectionality/

Shalka, T. R. (2019a). Mapping the intersections of gender and college trauma. *International Journal of Qualitative Studies in Education, 32*(6), 560–575. https://doi.org/10.1080/09518398.2019.1597207

Shalka, T. R. (2019b). Trauma and the interpersonal landscape: Developmental tasks of the relational self identity site. *Journal of College Student Development, 60*(1), 35–51. https://doi.org/10.1353/csd.2019.0002

Shalka, T. R. (2022). Nurturing a trauma-informed student affairs division. *About Campus, 27*(2), 18–25. https://doi.org/10.1177/10864822221100253

Shalka, T. R., & Leal, C. C. (2022). Sense of belonging for college students with PTSD: The role of safety, stigma, and campus climate. *Journal of American College Health, 70*(3), 698–705. https://doi.org/10.1080/07448481.2020.1762608

Substance Abuse and Mental Health Services Administration [SAMHSA]. (2014). *SAMHSA's concept of trauma and guidance for a trauma-informed approach* (HHS Publication No. (SMA) 14-4884). Substance Abuse and Mental Health Services Administration. https://ncsacw.samhsa.gov/userfiles/files/SAMHSA_Trauma.pdf

van der Kolk, B. A. (2014). *The body keeps the score: Brain, mind, and body in the healing of trauma.* Viking.

Venet, A. S. (2021). *Equity-centered trauma-informed education.* W. W. Norton & Company.

White House Task Force to Protect Students from Sexual Assault. (2017, January). *Preventing and addressing campus sexual misconduct: A guide for university and college presidents, chancellors, and senior administrators.* https://obamawhitehouse.archives.gov/sites/obamawhitehouse.archives.gov/files/images/Documents/1.4.17.VAW%20Event.Guide%20for%20College%20Presidents.PDF

4

PERSONAL PRACTICES FOR TRAUMA-INFORMED STUDENT AFFAIRS WORK

Although trauma-informed practice is sometimes about shaping systems and things external to us, it's also about fostering ways of being that guide how we move through the world. We ultimately need both. As Gloria Anzaldúa has stated, "I change myself, I change the world" (Anzaldúa, 2012, p. 92). Who we are shapes what our world becomes. Thus, viewing ourselves as instruments of change toward trauma-informed practice becomes a powerful position from which to work.

In the previous chapter, I discussed spheres of influence as a place to ground our energies in informing trauma-informed practice. This chapter focuses on what is squarely in our own control in this work—the personal actions we as student affairs educators can engage in to build a trauma-informed practice. First, I will discuss some of the useful attitudes (or ways of being), skills, and knowledge bases that student affairs practitioners need to develop in supporting college student survivors of trauma. Next, I will unpack the secondary impacts of exposure to others' traumas and the importance of self-care.

Recognizing Our Impact

As explained in previous chapters, trauma doesn't stay contained within the boundaries of those primarily impacted. Trauma ripples through relationships and communities and extends well beyond the individuals and communities who were initially affected by traumatic experiences (Shalka, 2019). Trauma finds a way of showing up in relationships and interactions whether with those we're close to or those who are just acquaintances. Trauma inevitably finds a way to resist being siloed.

Thus, an important starting point in our trauma-informed work is recognizing our impact. Whether we're personally impacted by trauma or interacting with those who have been, the ways in which we show up with each other are at the core of a trauma-informed approach. In essence, we need to begin asking ourselves a version of the question: *How do the ways I move through the world impact those around me who have survived trauma (including myself if applicable)?*

Let me offer an example to add texture to this question. During the COVID-19 pandemic, I, like many other educators around the world, was interacting with numerous students and colleagues who were struggling with all that was happening. At various points, I was struggling too. In those times of struggle, I needed grace from others, so that is what I tried to extend in return. I was conscience of leading with that grace in my classrooms and recall one student who both needed and appreciated it during this time frame. She was struggling with getting assignments completed and sometimes not showing up to class. I kept checking in and asking whether she was ok as my entry point before I got to anything about assignments or the course itself. She was appreciative of the grace but also expressed that she wished I knew her at a different time in her life because she was usually a very strong student and on top of her game and she knew that wasn't what she'd been presenting to me in my course. I reassured her that I already knew that from stories from my colleagues, and I recognized this was just a difficult period and not indicative of her capacities as a student. To make a long story short, she struggled throughout the semester but I kept meeting her with compassion and grace. She ultimately confided in me that she was dealing with trauma in her life and expressed that she felt I could be understanding because of what I study. We had to work out some alternatives along the way, but she was able to finish the semester strong.

I'm not going to pretend that my interactions with this student alleviated her traumatic experiences. I do hope that our interactions, at the very least, didn't add additional burdens to an already difficult period for her. This is just one example of how the ways in which we carry ourselves can impact a student who has experienced trauma, and it happened to be a positive one. But, I would be remiss if I didn't share that not all of my student interactions have been that way.

Even as someone who studies trauma and strives to bring that lens to my interactions with others, I miss opportunities to see trauma under the surface and I do harm in the process. In a different example, I was working with a student who presented challenge after challenge to me in terms of our interactions. I became especially frustrated when I came to learn that not only was this student treating me disrespectfully, but that the student was interacting in similarly disrespectful ways with some of my colleagues and other students. Unfortunately, that dynamic is a real trigger point for me, and it led me to get increasingly frustrated with this student and less and less capable of maintaining a stance of grace. I learned much later that this student had a traumatic experience that was likely under the surface of their interactions with me and others. Trauma is certainly not an excuse to treat others with disrespect, but it did provide me with additional information to better understand an explanation for why this student was interacting as they were. Or, at least a *possible* explanation. The bottom line was that I missed it, and I missed an opportunity to be a supportive person in this student's life. My interactions likely did not make the student's traumatic experience any worse, but, perhaps, my increasing stance of frustration rather than care and curiosity did add additional burdens to this student's experience.

In short, the way we show up with others impacts them and their potential experiences of trauma. We won't always know that trauma is present. We won't always be able to maintain a stance of grace and care, because we're human. Regardless, the capacity to keep striving for that grounded presence and compassion and grace is what we must keep working toward. In this way, trauma-informed practice is so much more than just offering resources or educating ourselves about trauma. It is a way of being and a continuous practice that we must engage in.

Approaching Trauma-Informed Practice as a Way of Being

It might be helpful for me to first explain what I mean by "way of being" before we get too far. This is a term that means different things in different places. The way I am using it here is to denote the difference between a superficial adoption of trauma-informed practices versus one that is embraced and lived across our decisions and actions. Trauma-informed practice is a buzzword in many communities right now, but I'm advocating for a student affairs practice that moves beyond the glitz and glamour of what's trendy, to instead one that is deeply infused and beneficial to our students and colleagues in years to come. It's great to attend a workshop on trauma-informed practice or engage in reading about it as a staff, but then what? I'm less interested in the pats on the back we like to give ourselves for being trained in trauma-informed practice and much more interested in what are we doing with that training to improve the lives of the members of our communities and the practices we collectively engage in. Thus, when I say we're approaching trauma-informed practice here as a way of being, I'm talking about taking up the call to live this work. I'm asking that we commit ourselves to developing a lens on our interactions and practices that make it impossible for us not to see how trauma can impact relationships and communities. I'm asking that we commit to infusing this lens into everything we do in campus communities. I'm asking that we begin to see trauma-informed practice as a way of being that transforms how we show up with one another. It's a tall order *and* an important one. Below, I offer three ways of being that can further our capacities to approach our work and relationships through a trauma-informed lens: (1) nurturing a sense of humanness; (2) seeing those impacted by trauma as whole beings; and (3) arriving with compassionate curiosity.

Way of Being #1: Nurturing a Sense of Humanness (for Ourselves and Others)

Student affairs is a people-oriented profession. So many of us have stories about how and why we entered the profession that ultimately come back to people whether it be an important mentor who helped us see something in ourselves or a desire to "meet students where they are" and support their growth and development in college. This people orientation is a good starting point in our work toward trauma-informed practice and offers a solid foundation to build upon.

In nurturing a trauma-informed way of being, we need to then go deeper. We need to build on being inspired by others or wanting to be supportive to others and start digging into commitments to *really* seeing others and honoring others for their humanity, first and foremost.

Many of our social contexts work against this goal. It seems easy to say we can strive to see the humanity in others as our primary lens, but there are many social conditioning mechanisms that make this harder to do in practice. Consider some of these examples that can lead us to consciously or unconsciously dehumanize our colleagues and students:

- We're routinely in systems of limited resources in higher education and sometimes a perceived competition for those limited resources. Scarcity mindsets make it easier to bare down in protecting who and what we perceive to be "our own."
- Systems of oppression implicitly and explicitly shape our actions and interactions in higher education environments, and work to keep some people out and/or invisible. The microaggressions that undergird many of our campus interactions delineate who is "part of" and who is not. These systems also clearly remind those of us who are "not part of" that these systems were never built with us in mind.

Thus, our first task in a trauma-informed way of being is to nurture a humanizing stance. Nurturing this stance means that we bring our attention back to the wholeness and humanity of others. We see others as doing their best to achieve their goals, even when those actions are different than how we might achieve the same. We see in others a desire for meaning and fulfillment. We see our colleagues and students as filled with the same mixture of fears and dreams, strengths and stumbles as we ourselves embody. Yet, at the same time, we embrace not the Golden Rule (Do To Others What You Would Want), but in the words of one of my mentors, Deborah Golder, the Platinum Rule—Do to Others as They Would Want for Themselves. This is a nuanced but important shift that can hold the reality of inequities in our world without further reproducing them.

Dr. Martin Luther King, Jr. spoke of *the Beloved Community* (The King Center, n.d.). It is an aspirational concept, to be sure, but one that King believed was achievable. The Beloved Community is one where we recognize our mutual humanity to the point that we're unable to accept the suffering of others in any form. We become unwilling to leave anyone behind. It doesn't mean that we no longer hold people accountable or that conflicts no longer arise, but we're committed to resolving conflicts with one another through love and nonviolence.

That feels lofty in the context of student affairs practice, perhaps, but also maybe not. What would it mean to commit to nonviolence, for example, in our practice? Let's imagine the microviolences we might create in our practice. It could be a dismissive response to a student, writing a colleague off in our heads even if we don't say it out loud, pushing our own agenda without consideration of others, or even beating ourselves up over a decision we made. These may feel like small things, but they collectively add up to deteriorating effects in our communities. When we consider, then, what it might mean to adopt a stance of humanity in our practice, it begins first and foremost in these small, individual moments where we can seek to lead with love and embrace the beautiful imperfection and complexity of those with whom we interact (including ourselves). From that nonviolent humanizing stance, we can hold one another (and ourselves) with grace and honor our shared humanity.

Way of Being #2: Seeing Those Impacted by Trauma as Whole Beings

Trauma-informed practice attunes us to the potential of trauma and its impacts, which is what we want it to do. However, as Ginwright (2018) observes, a limitation of trauma-informed practice is when we focus on the individual's trauma at the expense of seeing that person as a whole being. Ginwright likens this approach to a deficit-based model in that when we focus exclusively on an individual's trauma we're essentially communicating to that person "you are the worst thing that ever happened to you" (Ginwright, 2018, para. 6).

I've observed in my own research how this approach to trauma may be a mismatch for what those who have experienced trauma may ultimately need. In Chapter 2, I introduced my past research participant, Beth's, metaphor of the sapling in the hurricane to describe her sense of self after trauma—she was impacted by the experience, certainly, but it wasn't the sole definer of who she was in the world. She described the sapling that grows in the hurricane as having a little bump on it that is a reminder of the trauma, but the tree still grows strong. I love that metaphor as a reminder that there's more to anyone's story or experience than just their trauma. It doesn't mean that trauma doesn't take on heightened salience in someone's life at various points. Certainly, there are times when trauma can be all-consuming. However, the trauma is never everything and all a person is and that is what Ginwright's (2018) work draws attention to by suggesting that we expand and build beyond deficit-focused trauma-informed practice to instead a holistic mindset and approach focused on *healing centered engagement*.

Thus, a key way of being in our trauma-informed work is holding onto holism. It means that while we become attuned to trauma in our interactions with others, we simultaneously are attuned to all the other pieces of others' experiences. We're attentive to the constellation of their social identities, the myriad experiences they have had in their lives, and the ways in which they have been strong, hopeful, and filled with possibilities. As Ginwright (2018) explains, this approach encourages us toward restoration and an emphasis on "what's right with you" (para. 12).

As we attune ourselves to this holism, it also means attention to systemic oppression. As mentioned in previous chapters, trauma is often produced and/or amplified in the context of systems of oppression. Developing our capacities to see others as whole beings also means that we need to recognize both individual and systemic factors impacting trauma, including the systemic origins of certain traumas. It means that we work to restore individuals and communities while we're simultaneously committed to dismantling systems of power and oppression that create trauma in the first place. This work is interconnected.

Way of Being #3: Arriving With Compassionate Curiosity

One of my mentors, Dr. Jen Gilbride-Brown, has worked in the space of critical service learning. One of her mantras that I often hear bouncing around in my head is "nobody is broken!" When preparing students for service learning abroad, this was one of her constant refrains to remind us of a tendency in those spaces to view others as at a deficit in some way and that we're rushing in with our American savior mentality to save them, but that, in fact, we should be engaging in mutuality. The people who are best equipped to identify and solve problems are more often than not those who are living the experience firsthand.

A parallel savior logic can develop in trauma-informed practice when we're not attentive to it. It can be deceptively easy to slip into a stance of problem-solver, fixer, and advice giver extraordinaire that can be subconsciously rooted in a personal sense of knowing best. In fact, that's precisely what many of us in educational settings have been well-trained to do whether implicitly or explicitly. We're taught how to critique and poke holes and figure out what's not working and then propose solutions.

Sometimes when we're working with others who have endured trauma, they do need help fixing something or receiving advice. A student who is sharing that they're homeless and need resources may well be telling us that information because they would like our assistance in helping to connect them with resources and supports. A student who is deciding about whether to press charges against someone who has physically assaulted them may well be asking for our advice about what to do because they have come to value our insight.

However, most interactions we may have with individuals who have survived trauma may not be directed toward resources and advice. Instead, very often what trauma survivors are asking of us (whether explicitly or implicitly) is the kind of support that comes from a humbleness of presence. Back to the "nobody is broken" mantra, when we're approaching our work through a trauma-informed lens we're trying to nurture our capacities to provide the kind of presence where we pay attention to what the other person needs and is actually asking of us, rather than slipping into behaviors like unsolicited advice giving that signal we are seeing others as predominantly "broken" or needing to be fixed. There is humility in that kind of presence because it's explicitly not about us but rather about the person in front of us.

When I'm doing workshops about trauma-informed practice, I often tell participants that if there's one thing they take away from our time together, it's that I hope they can implant the following question into their heads: *"What else might be going on?"* This question isn't about diagnosing or being an investigator. The question is a memory device to remind us that what we see on the surface may not be the full story. It's a reminder that sometimes what presents as challenging behavior or frustrating situations may have an undercurrent that we're not aware of. It's fundamentally about opening ourselves up to holding others with grace. As one of my counselor friends has told me many times before, "No one wakes up in the morning asking 'How can I mess up my life today?'" Yet, we're primed to make all kinds of snap judgments about others' behavior that leads us to the conclusion that that is exactly someone's goal. *"What else might be going on?"* helps us to unwind those subconscious or even pre-conditioned responses.

We can lean on that question to dislodge our patterns of interaction and to open ourselves up to complexity in others. But then what? What can we fill the space of that opening up with? This takes us to our third way of being toward a trauma-informed practice which is that of developing a stance of compassionate curiosity in our interactions with others.

Curiosity about others invites a sense of humbleness. It reminds us that we don't always know everything that others are encountering in their lives, but that we can work to slow down, listen, and observe to enrich our understanding. Sofer (2018) defines empathy as "an intuitive reaching to understand another's experience on its own terms" (p. 99). What helps to guide our intuitive reach toward understanding is curiosity. Our capacity to lead with curiosity in our interactions with others is what allows space for alternate perspectives or interpretations and the potential to understand why and how others are moving through the world as they are. That is critical from a trauma-informed perspective because trauma impacts how we move through the world in profound ways. For example, maybe the person who seems withdrawn and standoffish may be perceived as a snob, but maybe that person is actually trying to work through a triggering experience. Or to offer another example, maybe the person who gets easily fired up in a meeting or seems to lash out at others is interpreted as trying to derail a process, but maybe they're actually feeling overwhelmed and out of control in the space because of a trauma history. Curiosity offers us the potential of holding space for the latter possibilities in both examples.

Compassion offers us direction and guidance on how to engage our curiosity. It invites us toward the person and their humanity, first and foremost. It orients our sense of curiosity to be rooted in our care for the other person and a desire for their well-being as opposed to any needs to diagnose or figure someone out. Most importantly, compassion anchors us firmly in trying to approach others with grace and a desire to reduce the capacity for harm in our interactions.

I really appreciate a definition of compassion that is offered by clinical psychologist, Dr. Christopher Germer. He shares that "compassion is love plus suffering . . . when love meets suffering and stays loving, that's compassion" (Brown, 2022). He goes on to share that when we encounter pain and suffering it can take us away from love because we can easily lean into fear or anger or disgust. But compassion means that we stay with that place of love in the face of pain.

This is such a beautiful description of the kind of compassionate presence we're trying to foster in trauma-informed work because trauma is exactly the kind of suffering that can induce fear or anger or disgust. Yet, our practice can be that of staying with—staying with loving presence and gentle curiosity for another. It means leaning into the discomfort and the fear that might come up for us in the presence of others' traumas and giving space for the possibility of trauma undergirding difficult situations rather than labeling a person as a problem for an outburst that could be rooted in a sense of unsafety after trauma. Staying with love in the face of pain is that compassionate curiosity in which we're better able to be attentive to those with whom we're interacting in ways that honor their agency.

Developing Knowledge and Skills

I've often asked participants in my research studies what advice they may have for administrators and faculty to better support students who may be navigating traumatic experiences. Amira shared a perspective with me that really gets to the heart of the matter. Her advice was essentially asking administrators and faculty to take the time to do the work—she wanted campus officials to be well trained in diversity and equity as a starting point to really see and understand students alongside work to provide resources and maintain a stance of openness. Fundamentally, she was asking to be seen. Amira stressed the following as important in terms of how administrators and faculty should interact with students who have experienced trauma:

> That when [students] do bring those issues to you, that you are not invalidating their experiences. That's what I've seen from a lot of administrators is that even if it's not a concern to you or if you are limited in your ability to respond, it's really, really important for students who report to you, or who come to you for assistance, that you don't invalidate their lived experiences. Because it may not be important to you, but from the student's perception it is super, super important to them. It can significantly impact whether they reach out to somebody else because it takes a lot of courage to reach out . . . when you come across an administrator or professional who completely invalidates it even more so, that is absolutely crushing.

Invalidation of students can happen for a variety of reasons. Often, I think it is less about administrators and faculty intentionally trying to invalidate a student's experience as much as not having the knowledge and tools to understand what is happening. Or, perhaps, it happens because faculty and administrators are stretched too thin and have to move quickly as a result. That said, the reason becomes rather irrelevant when the impact for the student is ultimately detrimental or "absolutely crushing" as Amira articulates.

The three key ways of being that I've discussed earlier are the solid ground upon which we can build other things in our trauma-informed practices to be able to effectively validate and support students who have experienced trauma. I see those ways of being as necessary starting points that we can use as scaffolds to help support additional tools. The next step involved is developing some knowledge and skills as tools to attach onto that scaffold. I want to emphasize the -ing part of the "developing" that I just named. This work is active and ongoing. It's not as simple as attending a workshop and crossing that off the list. Trauma-informed practice is one that involves a broader commitment to ongoing and sustained learning. Although more specifics about the knowledge and skills we can use to bolster our trauma-informed practice are delineated in more detail in other chapters, I want to use the space below to highlight some of the components that we might want to keep on our radars.

Knowledge

In Chapters 1 and 2, I provided information about what trauma is and how it might show up in the lives of college students. There's a lot to learn and metabolize. Let me summarize some of the key pieces of information that are important to carry forward in our practices as student affairs educators. First, trauma-informed practice is keenly attentive to the reality that trauma is prevalent (SAMHSA, 2014). We must assume that in any group we enter, there are people present who have been impacted by trauma. Having that lens on our interactions has the potential to soften how we interact with one another and create space for mutual grace and understanding. Second, our knowledge base has to be informed by the intersecting roles of systems of power and oppression. To refer back to Amira, part of the challenge she faced in her campus environment was due to the fact that she felt her experiences of trauma (discrimination and physical assault due to her identity as a Muslim woman, and body shaming) were invisible in many ways, because of a lack of a diversity and equity lens on student experiences of trauma. Discrimination in Amira's campus environment amplified her traumatic experience. Meanwhile, Amira never really knew where to go for support in the way that she felt she might if her trauma was sexual assault. Foregrounding power and oppression in our trauma-informed work allows us to expand our understanding of what trauma is and recognize the ways in which systems of power are both the sources and amplifiers of many traumatic experiences. It directs our attention in a trauma-informed system to the work we must simultaneously do to dismantle systems of privilege. Finally, it is important that we see trauma in terms of its nature toward multiplicity rather than simplicity. Trauma impacts both individuals and communities across multiple layers of experience (Shalka, 2019). Trauma is interwoven with our social identities and our relative positions within systems of power. Trauma can be both named and silenced, embraced and shunned.

Skills

In the chapters to come, I will dive deeper into many specific skills that will help to support work with students as well as within larger organizational structures that frame higher education. One of the most critical elements that undergirds many important skills in a trauma-informed practice is closely connected to the ways of being already presented. The way we show up for others is the backbone of this work that acts as the foundation and scaffold for specific trauma-informed skills. These tools and skills include things such as active listening, relationship-building, decisions and actions that help to restore safety and control, and embracing silence. Our evolving tool kit must also include practical elements such as connecting students with resources, while doing so mindfully and thoughtfully. Finally, an important skill that has already been mentioned and will resonate in many other ways throughout the book is to get in the habit of asking "*What else might be going on?*" in the interactions we have with others. Honing our capacities to slow down and leave space for possibilities of trauma and healing is a key skill for trauma-informed work.

Secondary Traumatic Stress

Many genesis stories about why people get into the field of student affairs have common roots. If we were doing a thematic analysis of the stories, we'd likely hear themes of students and relationships emerging. Sometimes, student affairs professionals speak of the amazing experiences they had as undergraduates and how they want to pay it forward. Sometimes, student affairs professionals speak of the difficult or challenging experiences they had as undergraduates and how they want to do better for other students to come. At the root of many stories is the desire to support students.

Student affairs is fundamentally about supporting students. We hear emphases on being "student-centered," "meeting students where they're at," and "nurturing the whole student." The students who are met with this blanket of support are in very good hands from many exemplary student affairs professionals. However, it's not exclusively a good thing, and the balance of taking care of others while ensuring we ourselves are ok is a delicate one. Layer on that institutional structures that keep nudging us to do more with fewer and fewer resources and the environment is ripe for difficulties. In an edited volume, Sallee (2020) and contributors make the case that student affairs practice is unsustainable for professionals with frequent examples of how it strains professionals' well-being. One part of that strain and compromise is the potential for secondary traumatic stress.

When we're working closely, empathetically, and frequently with others who have endured trauma or hardship, it can negatively impact us personally (van Dernoot Lipsky, 2009). That negative impact has many different terms that mean slightly different things from vicarious trauma to secondary traumatic stress. While both forms of secondary trauma result from direct empathetic engagement with others who have endured trauma, these terms represent different manifestations (Newell & MacNeil, 2010). Vicarious trauma is more focused on the cognitive level changes that might occur for a helper, including changes in terms of one's sense of safety or control in the world. Secondary traumatic stress, meanwhile, manifests in terms of outward behavioral changes that parallel symptoms of PTSD, such as being hypervigilant, being unable to sleep, or experiencing irritability and angry outbursts.

In her book, *Trauma Stewardship* Laura van Dernoot Lipsky (2009) discusses the related concept of a *trauma exposure response* and names it as "the ways in which the world looks and feels like a different place to you as a result of your doing your work" (p. 41) in relation to the suffering of others. van Dernoot Lipsky shares 16 different possible results of trauma exposure and notes that these can happen along a spectrum, where some changes could be unnoticeable while others may be dramatic. The 16 possible warning signs of trauma exposure include the following:

- Feeling helpless and hopeless
- A sense that one can never do enough
- Hypervigilance

- Diminished creativity
- Inability to embrace complexity
- Minimizing
- Chronic exhaustion/physical ailments
- Inability to listen/deliberate avoidance
- Dissociative moments
- Sense of persecution
- Guilt
- Fear
- Anger and cynicism
- Inability to empathize/numbing
- Addictions
- Grandiosity: An inflated sense of importance related to one's work

Many student affairs practitioners are primed for the kind of engagement with and exposure to students' traumas that could result in experiences of vicarious or secondary traumatic stress reactions. For example, student conduct professionals may be exposed to students' experiences of sexual violence, staff in residential life may respond to students' suicidal ideation or attempts, and advisors of student leaders may learn of students' experiences of racial trauma. The list goes on. It's clear from the descriptions above that when our exposure to others' traumas gets to a state of overwhelm, many aspects of our lives can be negatively implicated. From feeling unsafe in the world to being irritable or angry to losing our usual capacities for creativity and complexity, we must recognize that our empathetic engagements with the traumas of our students and colleagues must be approached mindfully. Otherwise, we suffer in ways that create harm for ourselves and those around us.

Taking Care of Ourselves

Years ago, while starting my dissertation research about college student trauma, I was aware of the potential that it could impact me in negative ways. I knew the topic was a difficult one and I went in prepared with what I thought was a good collection of self-care measures.

I was prepared that the material might be overwhelming and might even trigger me to my own experiences of trauma—I'd anticipated all of that. But, I was still met with curveballs along the way that I hadn't anticipated. I hadn't really considered what it might mean to be reading about trauma all day alongside interviewing and hearing about trauma firsthand. I hadn't considered the ways it would feel very isolating to hold the traumas of others in the context of a research study grounded in anonymity. I also hadn't anticipated the depth of emotions I would experience from deep pain and empathy for others to fear about how I was either helping or hurting. Collectively, the early parts of that research presented me with some wake-up calls when I realized my sleep was being impacted, I was stressed out, and I was feeling a general sense of lethargy in my body. I was made aware experientially of what I knew cognitively—trauma is embodied and it stays in the body until we find ways to release it. Over time, I've adopted better skills for how I engage with others' traumas.

Engagement with others' traumas is not an easy process, and student affairs professionals are frequently on the frontlines of these kinds of interactions. Similar to the ways my own body started to tell me my engagement was too much and I wasn't taking care of myself, student affairs professionals can speak to similar experiences of overwhelm in relation to the student traumas they encounter. In this section, I want to speak more to the "what can we do?" aspect of this reality. Let me be clear in stating that the work of self-care alongside exposure to trauma is not just an individual concern, it is (and should be) a systems one as well. Our organizational cultures very often like to promote self-care, and while self-care is necessary and I am a strong advocate of it, it is not enough. We cannot be asking student affairs professionals to self-care themselves back to wellness when they are embedded in organizational structures that themselves are antithetical to wellness (Shalka, 2022; Squire & Nicolazzo, 2019). In this section, I will discuss both prongs—self-care at an individual level as well as advocacy for institutional supports for wellness-centric practice and decision-making.

The Importance of Self-Care (and Some Words of Caution)

Being well is a fundamental piece of trauma-informed practice, because we simply cannot continue the work of supporting others' traumas and tending to our own when we're not ok. A much-used metaphor in helping professions is the airplane example—that you're supposed to put on your own oxygen mask before assisting others with theirs. The logic of airlines' approaches on this is that if you pass out because you don't have access to oxygen, you're literally useless to anyone around you let alone the fact that you're now in harm's way.

That metaphor is leaned on in helping professions because it's true—we can't be there as effective supports to others when we're depleted, overwhelmed, and stressed. This is obviously a given, even though there are many ways we fight that logic as educators or helpers. Sometimes, it's tempting to think we can just push through, and we'll rest at some later point down the road. Other times, it's equally tempting to feel like we are the only person in the world who can provide someone else what they need at this precise moment, so we'll just put our own needs on hold. Sometimes, we're just so in the habit of being everything to everyone that we can hardly get out of our own way to break the cycle and tend to ourselves. Sometimes, too, our organizations have put us in positions where we feel we have no other choice.

Self-care represents an important element of any work we do when we're engaging with others' traumas or our own (van Dernoot Lipsky, 2009; Venet, 2021). This is a place where we can be attentive to and honest with ourselves about how we're doing and take steps to heal, rest, and restore as needed. It's also a proactive space where we can put tools and practices in place in advance to help us maintain wellness and balance. Having those skills in place does not remove the difficulty of interacting with others' traumas or our own, but it does help us work with them in ways that can prevent further harm and sometimes even prove enriching.

I also believe and advocate that it's critical we engage in our own self-care not just as individual needs, but simultaneously because the more of us committed to radical self-care and healthy boundaries in our work lives, the more people around us will feel they have permission to do the same. In this sense, decisions toward personal wellness aren't just self-interested, but simultaneously about changing the culture of many organizations within which we work.

There is, however, a shadow side to self-care. The danger of self-care is less about problems for individuals who engage in it, and more so about organizations that push self-care as mechanisms to avoid confronting the harm they themselves are creating. Student affairs scholars Drs. Dian Squire and Z Nicolazzo (2019) wrote an article with the provocative subtitle *The Case Against Self-Care* that speaks to what I mean by this. What they unpack is the culture that seems increasingly pervasive in higher education of leaders and institutions demanding their employees (and student affairs professionals in particular) to do more and more with less and less. In the wake of these trends, self-care is pushed on employees to compensate for the toxic and neoliberal expectations that organizations are creating for employees. In other words, organizations are willing to over-work and under-value employees but offer yoga sessions and wellness days presuming that somehow makes up for it. Squire and Nicolazzo (2019) discuss this reality connected to expectations thrust on graduate assistants and put it much more bluntly:

> self-care rhetoric attempts to soften the harsh realities of capitalism that works to turn people's livelihoods, mental health, and social well-being into quantifiable output; it turns people into property to be used for institutional profit. It maximizes the amount of labor that a graduate student puts out while minimizing the need to authentically care about the "humanness" of a person. It is an epidemic in student affairs that dehumanizes students without attending to the systemic problems facing our field and the neoliberal university broadly. . . . To be clear, we are not arguing that self-care is bad. . . . We are arguing that self-care rhetoric devoid of fundamental shifts in how the field structures the work of graduate students is toxic and detrimental to the mental health of our students and the sustainability of the field.
>
> (p. 5)

I appreciate the caution that Squire and Nicolazzo's (2019) article raises. It's important to question things we see as assumed goods and recognize the limitations of those assumptions. In the case of self-care and trauma-informed practice, we have a *both/and* situation. Self-care is both critically important for us to engage *and* we must recognize how it is used to conceal the harms our organizations are creating. Below, I will offer some ideas about responding to this both/and by way of strategies we can engage personally to tend to our own wellness at the same time we advocate for institutional changes toward organizations that have wellness-centric decision-making as guiding principles.

Strategies of Self-Care

Self-care can be thought of as the actions (or inactions) we take to preserve or improve our well-being. Sometimes we jump to thinking about the tools of self-care (e.g., meditation, more sleep, etc.) without first thinking about the need. We have a variety of wellness needs in our lives that are important to identify before we rush to inserting the solution. Given that, I appreciate it when self-care is framed in terms of its multidimensionality. We can almost think of multiple wellness "buckets" that exist in our lives, and our goal is to make sure we're keeping all those buckets filled up. When they start to get empty, the effects of stress and strain may be felt more strongly.

Scott (2021) offers five such self-care buckets to consider along with several corresponding questions to reflect on in assessing how we're doing in that particular self-care dimension:

1. Physical
   Questions to consider: Are you getting enough sleep? Is your diet supporting your body well? Are you getting enough exercise?
2. Social
   Questions to consider: Are you getting enough face-to-face time with friends and family? How are you nurturing your relationships with friends and family?
3. Mental
   Questions to consider: Are you engaged in enough activities that mentally stimulate you?
   How are you proactively supporting your mental health?
4. Spiritual
   Questions to consider: Are you engaging in spiritual practices that you find fulfilling?

What questions do you ask yourself about your life and experience?

5. Emotional

Questions to consider: Do you have healthy ways to process your emotions? Do you incorporate activities into your life that help you feel recharged?

Taking the time to assess which of these self-care buckets might need some extra TLC then leads to a plan that will provide the right kind of support, including self-care strategies with both proactive and reactive components as needed. For example, someone might engage in meditation, running, and/or quality time with their family as ongoing and proactive measures of self-care. If they were to identify a period where they are feeling more stress than usual, some time to check in about their wellness buckets might reveal they are feeling particularly depleted physically, and then, they might add in some diet and/or sleep changes to further support their reactive self-care needs. Being able to hold the complexity of self-care as multidimensional and fluid helps to offer us the right kind of support we need to engage in that is individualized.

SOS Self-Care

Self-care works best when we're consistently attentive to it and view it as an ethos rather than a checklist. That said, there are inevitably times when we face immediate threats to well-being and need some immediate strategies to support us. What happens if we're working in residential life and have to travel to the hospital with a student who was hit by a car on campus? What happens if we're working in a student conduct office and sitting with a survivor of sexual assault detailing what happened to them? What happens if we're a senior student affairs administrator and a fire breaks out in one of the residence halls and we're working to relocate students to safe housing in the middle of the night? There are countless examples that student affairs professionals encounter that can prove personally destabilizing. We push through and get through in order to make sure students are ok, but that doesn't mean that once we've handled an immediate threat the next breath doesn't bring us a sense of overwhelm in our own bodies. In those moments of immediate self-care needs, the following SOS strategies might be useful:

1. Take a breath
   The breath is a powerful tool that's accessible to us. In times when we're feeling overwhelmed and/or anxious, the breath can help us find a balance between our sympathetic and parasympathetic nervous systems (van der Kolk, 2014). Focusing on extending the exhale, in particular, helps to activate the parasympathetic nervous system, which signals to our body that we are safe and able to calm down.
   Begin by taking a deep, slow inhale through the nose to a count of 4. Then engage in a long, slow exhale through slightly pursed lips to a count of 6 (the longer exhale is intentional to encourage further calming down). Pause at the end of the exhale then begin again when you are ready to take your next inhale. Continue this pattern with several more long, slow breaths. As you feel your body relaxing a bit more, begin to play with the possibility of lengthening the exhale by adding one count each at a time for several rounds of breath until you reach four counts on the inhale and eight counts on the exhale.
2. Reconnect with your body
   A sense of overwhelm or anxiety can feel like we're spinning out of control. One way to help ground ourselves out of those sensations is to focus our attention back to the body in specific ways. A particularly grounding focus can be drawing our attention to our feet (Emerson & Hopper, 2011).
   Whether you're sitting or standing, feel yourself planting your feet firmly on the ground. Allow your attention to focus on your feet. Begin by wiggling your toes around a bit. What does that feel like? Next, focus on what your feet and toes are touching—do you feel your toes rubbing gently against socks or your shoes or a carpet or even the air? What's the textural feeling of any of those things? Then, begin to feel the heaviness of your feet on the floor as you start to imagine roots growing out of the bottoms of your feet and deep into the ground beneath you.

As you imagine these deep roots growing, imagine feelings of groundedness, protection, and well-being in your body.
3. Connect with others
Our connections with others can also be sources of feeling grounded in the face of uncertainty or overwhelm. Isolation is a part of traumatic experience and exposure that can further amplify the difficult feelings we are experiencing (van der Kolk, 2014).
In those moments of SOS, connect. Talk with a trusted friend, loved one, therapist, or spiritual guide to be able to release some of the burden of overwhelm.

Pushing Our Systems Toward Wellness-Centered Decision-Making

Self-care is a necessary step in trauma-informed work, but it's also insufficient when we're embedded in systems that continue demanding more and more of us in ways that compromise our well-being. I see it as part of our personal sphere of influence to care for ourselves as best we can amid toxic systems and climates, while we simultaneously recognize we can't meditate or exercise away the impacts of some of those spaces.

I increasingly feel we're arriving at a moment of breakthrough in many of our organizational lives. Enough people are articulating the insufficiency of the status quo in ways that perhaps we will see micro changes and organizations that see their role as that of being wellness-centric for their students, staff, and faculty. As individuals, we may not have the magic wands to wave to insist on this change, but I believe our collective micro actions keep pushing at and nudging leaders and organizations in the right direction.

We can embark on that nudging in many ways. We can be the people who ask "Who were these spaces built for?" while demanding honest explorations and conversations about this question and action toward inclusion once we're honest in assessing who our current environments and practices leave out. We can embrace saying *no* to "opportunities" at work not as acts of defiance but as acts of love. As Brené Brown (2016) notes, the most compassionate people out there are the most boundaried people. We are able to love when we protect our energy and time in ways that we preserve the space and capacity to love. When we are in positions of power or influence, we can use that positionality to seek to relieve stress and strain from others. That might look like us as a supervisor who enforces a "no meetings week," so staff can catch up on other projects. That could look like chairing a search committee and providing candidates with interview questions in advance, so they have the chance to prepare rather than experience "gotcha" questions in the process. That might also look like asking a peer if you could send out communications for an upcoming program for them because that peer seems overwhelmed. These may all seem like small efforts that don't change an organizational culture, but of course, organizations are made up of individuals and the more of us who keep insisting on working in ways that support wellness, the closer we get to a tipping point of that becoming our new status quo.

Conclusion

This chapter emphasized the ways that our individual orientations and approaches are an important part of trauma-informed practice. Our ways of being exist as the scaffolds that we can then attach useful skills onto as we expand our capacities to work in trauma-informed ways. Though sometimes we can feel so small as an individual in a larger organization, there is tremendous power in that starting point. In the next few chapters, we will start expanding out from our individual ways of being and explore how we work directly with students who have been impacted by trauma as well as student leaders we work with who may be also doing that kind of support.

References

Anzaldúa, G. (2012). *Borderlands/La Frontera: The new mestiza* (25th anniversary, 4th ed.). Aunt Lute Books.

Brown, B. (2016). Brené Brown on empathy, compassion, and boundaries. *The Work of the People*. https://www.facebook.com/theworkofthepeople/videos/brené-brown-on-empathy-compassion-and-boundaries/10153967066765682/

Brown, B. (Host). (2022, November 30). The near and far enemies of fierce compassion, part 1 of 2. *Unlocking Us* [Audio podcast episode].

https://brenebrown.com/podcast/the-near-and-far-enemies-of-fierce-compassion-part-1-of-2/

Emerson, D., & Hopper, E. (2011). *Overcoming trauma through yoga: Reclaiming your body*. North Atlantic Books.

Ginwright, S. (2018, May 31). The future of healing: Shifting from trauma informed care to healing centered engagement. *Medium*. https://ginwright.medium.com/the-future-of-healing-shifting-from-trauma-informed-care-to-healing-centered-engagement-634f557ce69c

The King Center. (n.d.). *The King philosophy—Nonviolence 365®*. https://thekingcenter.org/about-tkc/the-king-philosophy/

Newell, J. M., & MacNeil, G. A. (2010). Professional burnout, vicarious trauma, secondary traumatic stress, and compassion fatigue. *Best Practices in Mental Health*, *6*(2), 57–68. https://doi.org/10.1007/s41542-019-00045-1

Sallee, M. W. (2020). *Creating sustainable careers in student affairs: What ideal worker norms get wrong and how to make it right*. Stylus.

Scott, E. (2021, December 9). 5 self-care practices for every area of your life. *Verywell Mind*. https://www.verywellmind.com/about-us-5184564

Shalka, T. R. (2019). Navigating the complex space of supporting student survivors of trauma. In P. M. Magolda, M. B. Baxter Magolda, & R. Carducci (Eds.), *Contested issues in troubled times: Student affairs dialogues on equity, civility, and safety* (pp. 221–232). Stylus.

Shalka, T. R. (2022). Nurturing a trauma-informed student affairs division. *About Campus*, *27*(2), 18–25. https://doi.org/10.1177/10864822221100253

Sofer, O. J. (2018). *Say what you mean: A mindful approach to nonviolent communication*. Shambhala.

Squire, D. D., & Nicolazzo, Z. (2019). Love my naps, but stay woke: The case against self-care. *About Campus*, *24*(2), 4–11. https://doi.org/10.1177/1086482219869997

Substance Abuse and Mental Health Services Administration [SAMHSA]. (2014). *SAMHSA's concept of trauma and guidance for a trauma-informed approach* (HHS Publication No. (SMA) 14-4884). Substance Abuse and Mental Health Services Administration. https://ncsacw.samhsa.gov/userfiles/files/SAMHSA_Trauma.pdf

van der Kolk, B. A. (2014). *The body keeps the score: Brain, mind, and body in the healing of trauma*. Viking.

van Dernoot Lipsky, L. (2009). *Trauma stewardship: An everyday guide to caring for self while caring for others*. With C. Burk. Berrett-Koehler.

Venet, A. S. (2021). *Equity-centered trauma-informed education*. W. W. Norton & Company.

5
SUPPORTING STUDENTS WHO HAVE EXPERIENCED TRAUMA

Trauma feels overwhelming because by definition it is. Supporting others through trauma can also feel overwhelming. Sometimes, it feels overwhelming because it is physically and emotionally demanding. At other times, the act of supporting feels overwhelming for less concrete reasons, such as when we're unsure where to begin and worry that nothing we do will make any meaningful difference for those who are enduring traumatic experiences.

It's true that there are no magic wands to wave in this work that make survivors' pain go away. However, it's also true that some of the simplest efforts are those that hold tremendous power. Dr. Rachel Naomi Remen (2006) offers that "the most basic and powerful way to connect to another person is to listen. Just listen. Perhaps the most important thing we ever give each other is our attention. And especially if it's given from the heart" (p. 143). In other words, our most powerful support can be as simple as how we show up with others and how we listen—the meaningful difference happens in those simple acts.

In this chapter, I provide many tools and pathways forward in supporting college students who have survived trauma, but let me be clear that this work remains fundamentally about *who we are* with student survivors more than anything else—those ways of being from the previous chapter continue to hold true. Resources will always have a place, but the most fundamental work is that of presence and humanity. As the quote from Dr. Remen suggests, our most important work may well come through our attention in listening to survivors, inviting them with us away from isolation and back to connection.

DOI: 10.4324/9781003444435-6

Framing the Scope of Our Work Supporting Student Survivors of Trauma

Outside of trained counselors, social workers, and the like in clinical practice with students, most of us in student affairs or adjacent roles are not interacting with students in therapeutic settings. It may go without saying that if we're not in a therapeutic setting with a student, then we aren't supposed to function as a counselor to them, but it bears repeating. Because student affairs is a helping profession and many practitioners have training in basic helping and/or counseling skills, it never hurts to be reminded that we're not counselors unless explicitly trained as such and working explicitly that way with a student in a therapeutic relationship.

What does our work entail, then? It's the everything else. We're present for students to support them as fellow humans who may be struggling. We're there to offer resources, but ultimately to trust student survivors as adults with agency to make decisions about what will be best for them. We're there to offer compassion and presence, but also boundaries in knowing where our own limits are and why.

My research participants have shared immense wisdom with me over the years about what they wish administrators and faculty on their campuses knew about their experiences and how to support them. It often boils down to asking to be understood, trusted as experts of their own experiences, and approached with humanity. When I asked one participant, Violet, this question she articulated a rub that many of us working in higher education are challenged by too—institutions can fall into the trap of dehumanizing students as revenue streams or risks to manage, at the expense of remembering there are real people's lives in the mix. What Violet ultimately wants from institutions and institutional actors is quite simple and straightforward:

> I think the best way for a university to handle it is to say here are the resources, you can use them or not. I am here for you. I care about you. If you were ever in physical danger or emotional danger or feel that you're going to endanger yourself, please let me know because I care about you. I don't care about you as an investment or as an asset. I care about you as a person.

It seems straightforward as Violet captures it, but there's a lot of complexity in those statements, too. Underneath her words are several values requests. For example, she's asking us to treat students as adults with agency as opposed to assuming we know better. She's asking us to be prepared for students, while knowing that support isn't a one-size-fits-all. She's also asking us to remember the person in front of us as opposed to getting caught up in policies and bureaucracies. Following Violet's suggestions, in the remainder of this chapter, I will explore some tangible practices that offer the kinds of support students need as fellow humans, rather than as neoliberal constructions of paying customers or even nameless and faceless credit hours.

Specific Practices to Support Students Who Have Experienced Trauma

In the previous chapter, I offered several ways of being that serve as the solid ground and scaffolds for our trauma-informed work. In this chapter, I'm now shifting to talking more about some of the tangible practices, considerations, and tools we need to draw on in directly supporting students who have experienced trauma. Below, I offer six practices that I see as cornerstones to this work, including the following:

1. Nurturing relationships
2. Being present
3. Addressing issues of safety and control
4. Attending to the complications of disclosure
5. Providing resources and support mindfully
6. Holding space for growth, resilience, and recuperation

Supporting Students Practice #1: Nurturing Relationships

As was mentioned in Chapter 2, relationships are a critical and complex component of traumatic experiences. Numerous studies demonstrate that empathetic relationships play a fundamental role in how survivors of trauma heal and recuperate (van der Kolk, 2014). However, relationships are also very complicated in the aftermath of trauma. As sociologist Dr. Kai Erikson (1995) eloquently captures, "trauma has both centripetal and centrifugal tendencies. It draws one away from the center of group space while at the same time drawing one back" (p. 186). Many of my past research participants have articulated a push-and-pull that can develop after traumatic experience—sometimes survivors desperately need others for support, while other times survivors need to push others away to regain their independence or because they feel isolated or alienated by others who may not understand what they have endured (Shalka, 2019b).

The importance and the challenges of relationships after trauma speak to why relationships become a key feature of trauma-informed work (e.g., Shalka, 2022; Venet, 2021). Thus, attention to building empathetic and authentic relationships with students must be a priority to effectively support survivors. Importantly, relationships should be established long before trauma potentially occurs, so that students have connections and supportive others to turn to when they need them. One of my participants, Amira, talked about the challenges she had in knowing who to go to on her college campus in relation to her trauma. She shared that if she had been sexually assaulted it was more clear, but given her trauma did not fit in that box, she was left not knowing who might be helpful to her. Additionally, Amira had several experiences of being discriminated against or not listened to on her campus from staff (including being followed and stopped by the campus police, watching how concerns about discrimination and bullying against a trans* friend of hers were ignored, and being dismissed at the health center in relation to concerns she was presenting with). In short, Amira had no obvious places on her campus for support through her trauma and ample reasons to assume her situation would not have been understood.

Trauma-informed work means that completely aside from traumatic experience, we're attentive to ensuring every student has the opportunity to develop trusting, empathetic, and validating relationships with staff and/or faculty. Focused attention on relationship and community building is hardly a new concept for student affairs professionals. We know how to do this well by creating programs and interactions that "meet students where they are" and invite students' full selves and histories into the spaces in which they engage. What might be new is why this matters in the presence of trauma. Relationships aren't simply connected to student engagement and persistence. In the case of trauma, they are connected to safety, control, recuperation, and well-being.

We need to conceptualize relationship building as an imperative for student well-being. That imperative must also be recognized as an equity issue, because inevitably our campuses are structured in ways that make it easier for some students to be in meaningful relationship with faculty and staff than for others. We may be deeply connected to student leaders, but are we finding equal ways to connect with general members of organizations? We may feel connected as educators to the students who seek us out to talk during breaks at a program or in a class, but are we also finding ways to make ourselves accessible and in relationship to those who are less likely to open themselves up in that way? Similarly, while we may have particular capacities in student affairs to create space for students to bring their whole selves, are we equally attentive to working to dismantle the systems of oppression that make many spaces unsafe and/or unwelcome to students with minoritized identities? These are the kinds of deeper commitments we need to engage in as we work toward supporting students who have survived trauma.

What are some examples of nurturing relationships?

- Consider the breadth of touchpoints particular staff or units have with students and who is being reached or not. Work through sociogram exercises with student affairs staff to better understand how individual professionals are connected to certain students or student groups across a campus. Look for patterns across all staff in a particular unit to identify places where that unit has strong relationships with certain groups of students, and where the unit needs to be more attentive to relationship building with particular students or groups of students.
- Invest in small efforts that go a long way, such as knowing students' names and pronouns, taking advantage of breaks during programs or trainings to go connect with a student we haven't before, and finding ways to be in spaces with students we may not usually be with to expand the reach of connections possible.

Supporting Students Practice #2: Being Present

Often, students come to us sharing experiences of trauma not out of a desire for us to fix something for them or even to offer them advice, but rather because they need space to share what has happened to them. A sometimes-overlooked aspect of traumatic experience is that it can have an isolating effect. One of my previous research participants, Liv, certainly harkened to this reality in articulating the way her traumatic experience meant she had outlived the collective experience of her friend group. I've also heard themes of isolation from participants like Paige. She shared a poignant scene with me about going star-gazing with some college friends one night after her traumatic experience. The star-gazing part was something they had collectively done many times before and she'd previously enjoyed, but that night, Paige struggled to enjoy the experience:

> I heard my friends around me, laughing at jokes that one was telling, and felt separated in that instance. I was envious that they could enjoy the moment and that they weren't weighed down with the type of thoughts I was feeling. I felt like they would never understand the struggle I was experiencing. . . . I felt that my trauma set me apart in the most negative of ways—making it impossible to relate to people on deeper levels, damaging my ability to trust those that were supposed to support and love me unconditionally, and making me question the decisions that had led me to that point.

> There wasn't much conversation that occurred that night—in general, these moments outdoors were a quiet escape for each of us. I think the lack of conversation increased my feelings of isolation. Going forward from that moment, I felt that if I were silent (or at the very least not communicating about my trauma or struggles) that I could belong in the group, and have a place, as long as I wasn't being authentic and hiding my pain.

Paige internalized a perceived lesson that to belong after trauma, she had to keep her trauma to herself. Part of why Paige and other survivors internalized that kind of message is because trauma is very often (whether consciously or unconsciously) not welcome in many social spaces. I think an underlying current of that reality is fear. Trauma triggers vulnerabilities in anyone who learns of the terrible things that can happen to fellow humans. Listening to the trauma of others, then, can make us uncomfortable—these are stories that are often difficult to hear, and difficult to sit with, and our temptation can be to turn away from them rather than stay with the discomfort on somebody's behalf. However, that is exactly what survivors are often asking of us—to just sit with them and be with them through the discomfort that is already their daily lived reality.

Being present is both simple and complicated to enact. It means being in the moment with a survivor, listening, supporting, and taking cues from them about what they need and how they want to proceed. The challenging part is that we're so well trained in student affairs to do anything but be present. We are trained to solve problems and provide resources and incorporate learning outcomes and teachable moments. Being present is asking us, instead, to not do, to not fix, and to not solve. It's asking us to just be and sit with and hold space for whatever a student survivor needs from us at that moment. Very often the need is simply to have another empathetic human in the world to be able to listen without judgment and fear. That kind of presence is what allows survivors to feel held and part of the social order again—it is the antidote to the kind of isolation that Liv and Paige articulated earlier.

What are some examples of being present for students who have survived trauma?

- Embrace silence. Many student affairs professionals have some training in basic counseling skills, and the use of silence may be one of the most powerful in that toolbox. Silence creates space for others and takes us out of fixing and solving mode and instead into simply being present mode.
- Listen to listen. Sometimes it's easy to get caught up in listening to speak rather than listening to actually listen and absorb what someone is sharing. For example, perhaps in meetings we're taking in information that others are sharing, but simultaneously building a list of rebuttals in our heads while they do. That's

listening to speak. Listening to listen is instead taking in the information to hear it and understand it on its own terms, without considering how we intersect it.

Supporting Students Practice #3: Addressing Issues of Safety and Control

Safety and control are basic human needs that are compromised by trauma. Traumatic experiences, by definition, challenge physical and/or psychological safety in the world. In ongoing traumatic circumstances, lack of safety may be a persistent concern, while even after event-based trauma, feelings of safety aren't instantly restored because the immediate danger has passed. Traumatic experiences have a way of re-tuning our stress response system and the world can feel unsafe in amplified ways (Perry & Winfrey, 2021; van der Kolk, 2014).

Feeling unsafe may be connected to related states of feeling out of control after trauma. Sometimes, trauma teaches survivors that they can't control the world around them and, consequently, the possibility of being harmed again looms large. Because trauma often seizes survivors' choices and safety, in the aftermath, survivors may become acutely focused on trying to control situations as mechanisms of self-protection. Connecting back to the wound metaphor from Dr. Gabor Maté that was introduced in Chapter 1, attempts to control may well be thought of as part of that scar tissue that he talks of—a means of trying to protect oneself from further harm. As a result, ensuring survivors have agency and control is of paramount importance. This is one reason that I and many other scholars and practitioners are against expansive mandatory reporting of sexual violence on college campuses because it takes control away from survivors, often doing more harm than good in the process (e.g., Freyd, 2016; Gómez, 2021; Holland et al., 2021). In essence, expansive mandatory reporting policies have the potential to re-traumatize survivors and re-create the kind of harm that was already inflicted in the original trauma.

Navigating campus environments and relationships can be particularly challenging for student survivors in light of these feelings of unsafety or lack of control. I've had the sense in talking with student survivors over the years that navigating campus environments after trauma can feel like a battleground. Take, for example, Ellie's experience after being sexually assaulted and facing constant anxiety and fear about the possibility of running into her assaulter on campus. She described some of these navigations in the following way:

> I always just felt this uneasiness that I was going to run into him. . . . He was in the Air Force ROTC . . . on Thursday the Air Force wore their uniforms to the lab. So from far away you can't see who it is because they're all wearing their Air Force hats or whatever. So you can't see who it is. And they walk in groups and they all look exactly the same, which I suppose is the purpose of a uniform . . . And I would like get so tense because I was like, "Oh shit, I can't tell if it's him from a certain distance away and I have to walk to that building to go to class, I'm going to have to pass them."

Many student survivors, like Ellie, are bracing for the "what if?" (in her case "What if I see the person who assaulted me?") and navigating campus environments and interactions that are filled with triggers, dangers, and discomforts. In essence, their abilities to feel safe and in control are routinely compromised. Given this, we have some complicated work to do in supporting students who have survived trauma in relation to safety and control. Reactively, we must ensure in the immediate aftermath of trauma with students (whether sexual assault or racial trauma or a campus shooting) that we're attentive to providing survivors with agency and control and work to re-establish a sense of immediate safety as quickly as possible. Proactively, ongoing work related to safety and control must be engaged in terms of fostering strong relationships, improving campus climate, and dismantling structural inequities. We must keep in mind that safety is felt or not in direct proportion to traumatization as well as our positionalities within systems of power and oppression. Thus, student support in terms of safety and control also means we actively dismantle the systems that contribute to inequity and amplify feelings of unsafety and lack of agency and control for individuals who embody minoritized identities.

What are some examples of addressing safety and control?

- In interactions with students, ensure there is choice and predictability. For example, in meetings, consider how predictable rhythms and patterns can be used so students know what to

expect from one interaction to another. If we're facilitating an activity, offer students options for how to engage.
- Consider the use of content/trigger warnings. We can't predict everything that could be triggering to a student, but paying attention to things that could be (such as a clip for a film about sexual violence, a reading about police violence toward Black people, etc.) and letting students know in advance about the content can provide them with choices about when and how and where they want to engage with the material.
- Engage in space audits. Take time to intentionally map out the spaces in which we engage with students focused around questions like: What images or symbols in this space communicate safety or unsafety? How does this space support comfort or discomfort? What interactions or routines that happen in this space can create harm or recuperation?

Supporting Students Practice #4: Attending to the Complications of Disclosure

Constructing a narrative account of what has happened is part of the healing process for many survivors of trauma. That narrative might include many things such as piecing together details of the traumatic experience or meaning making about what the trauma represents in the context of one's life moving forward. Sometimes, trauma can be experienced in a fragmented way (van der Kolk, 2014); thus, piecing a narrative back together again can bring the solace of a better understanding of what happened. Often, that process includes others, especially when those around a survivor remember details the survivor doesn't or have access to parts of the experience the survivor didn't. In my own experience of trauma, this was fundamental. I relied on doctors at the hospital, for example, to help tell me how I arrived to their unit and what I was like when I did (I had been put to sleep in the back of the ambulance and then into an induced coma so had a lot of missing time that I was trying to account for). I also relied on hearing from friends, family, faculty, and administrators at my university about how they learned of my accident, and how they started reacting.

All these pieces of the story proved critical to me in beginning to make sense of what had happened and trying to piece it together into the context of my life story.

However, as much as survivors may instinctively work to reconstruct an account of what they have endured, there are distinct complications related to this narrative building and ultimately narrative sharing. Specifically, we must be attentive to the complicated realities of disclosure for survivors after trauma. Participants in my research have told me just how complicated it can be for them to navigate disclosure, in terms of both disclosure they choose and disclosure that may be forced upon them.

To the former, participants have shared the difficulties of wanting to share their stories with others to connect, while struggling with assessments of when it's appropriate to share or not. Sometimes concerns about appropriateness are rooted in worries about how others will react. One of my participants, Lauren, struggled with figuring out the right balance because she wanted to share her traumatic experiences with others to feel authentically part of a community, but simultaneously, she was aware there was a time and place for that. She knew that disclosing her trauma too soon could keep her from being accepted in new communities. This is a balancing act that many student survivors of trauma wrestle with.

The other challenging part of disclosure can come through something I talk about as *forced disclosure*. This happens when a survivor feels like they have to share what happened to them even if they don't want to, and it can happen in many innocuous ways in the college environment. For example, health or other forms may require disclosures that students don't yet want to make. Or, we may have appeal policies in place for academics that essentially force students to disclose their trauma in hopes of salvaging a scholarship or grade. Or, we may engage in icebreaker activities in programs that compel a person to share something they're not ready to share. One of my research participants, Tyler, told me about how the visibility of his burn scars meant people sometimes asked him the really challenging question: "Do you mind if I ask what happened?" This would put Tyler into a difficult position where he often felt he had no choice, then, but to disclose what happened otherwise people would think he was rude and he'd have to navigate that interaction instead. But, he explained that people frequently didn't realize the impact of asking without a relationship first. As he shared "Usually I can talk about the accident without getting triggered, but depending on the space and the time, and who's around and how deep they go, I think people don't always recognize what they're digging up."

Tyler acknowledged the "double-edged sword" of disclosure—while it was often difficult for him when prompted by strangers it also pushed him forward in his recovery. There can indeed be benefits (mechanisms of healing, pathways to deeper connections with others [Tedeschi et al., 2018]) for survivors when they can disclose their traumatic experiences at a time that feels right, in a place that feels safe, and with those whom they feel connected to and are empathetic listeners. Yet, disclosure can also be difficult for student survivors and even harmful. Thus, we must proceed very mindfully and carefully given these possibilities. We need to pay attention to the ways in which we may (knowingly or unknowingly) be creating instances of forced disclosure for students that may be unwelcome and/or harmful to them. Ultimately, we don't need to know a student's particular trauma or details of what happened to support them and be compassionate and empathetic.

What are some examples of attending to the complications of disclosure?

- Review appeal and application processes to see whether they are inadvertently putting students into situations of forced disclosure. For example, if a student needs to describe why their grades fell to preserve a scholarship, is there an alternate process that could be engaged rather than a description that could include something related to trauma?
- When we're tempted to ask students details about why they need an accommodation, pause to consider whether we really need to know and/or what possibilities we might be creating for harmful instances of forced disclosure.

Supporting Students Practice #5: Providing Resources and Support Mindfully

Offering resources seems an obvious tool for supporting students who have experienced trauma. It's the piece many of us are well trained for and perhaps also an action that brings some immediate sense of comfort because it's tangible and helps us feel we have something to offer. That said, we sometimes lean on providing resources uncritically in ways that can be problematic in a couple of ways. First, resources, alone, may not constitute what survivors need to feel supported, and resources may not even be what a particular survivor wants. Second, providing resources is a decidedly reactive stance to trauma. It has its place, undeniably, but we also must remember that effective trauma-informed practice is equally proactive at the same time it is necessarily reactive. Finally, resources aren't neutral. There are ways our resources and/or the ways in which we offer them can produce further harm. We can, however, seek to provide resources and support thoughtfully and mindfully.

One element of providing resources and support mindfully is what I call *conscious referrals* (Shalka, 2019a). By conscious referrals, I'm asking that before we connect students to others or resources, we first think about why and what the implications of those actions might be. Take, for example, an administrator who is seemingly unable to sit with students in their difficulties and at the mention of anything remotely difficult or potentially traumatic, they instantly suggest the student make an appointment with the counseling center. That is one extreme. At the other extreme is an administrator who seems to be assuming the role of sole supporter to a student in distress, meeting with them constantly, and taking calls or texts day and night. That is another extreme.

What do these extreme examples offer? First, that things are not always what they appear and that is exactly why we need to be mindful about what we're doing. Maybe the first extreme example of the administrator who seems *under involved* and referring students too quickly is in fact doing so because their own personal trauma was being triggered and they knew it was harmful for them to continue the conversation with the student. That choice given that context may be appropriate. In the second example of seeming *overinvolvement*, perhaps there's more to the story there, too. Maybe that administrator is engaging in that kind of overinvolvement temporarily while also actively working to connect the student in other ways. Or maybe the obvious other people to connect the student with are somehow part of the original harm to the student, and that administrator is figuring out alternatives.

Second, both of those examples also offer examples of potentially harmful support that needs further consideration. The seemingly *under involved* administrator may be too quick to refer students elsewhere, which may lead to harm if students feel they're too much for others. This *under involvement* could also contribute to overburdening counseling centers when perhaps all the students needed was to share some of their stories with an empathetic listener and were not otherwise in distress. Similarly, the seemingly *overinvolved* administrator may be creating harm to both themselves and the student if they are leaning into a sense of martyrdom that may well burn them out and/or keep the student away from others who may be important in meeting their needs.

Another element of mindfully offering resources and support is related to coaching students to be their own best advocates, which is an important skill regardless of trauma history. Ultimately, there are limits to what we can do for students. Even when we can help, there are situations in which it's inherently better for a student to advocate on their own behalf. Thus, we foster self-advocacy but are available to step in when students need our help. We ultimately need to trust that students who have experienced trauma know what they need. I have seen far too many examples of institutional actors and processes foisting what they think is best upon students and, in the process, creating considerable harm. Trauma is fundamentally about losing control and agency in the world. Thus, when an institution starts to mandate what needs to happen next and/or what resources need to be offered or even pushed, there can be harm or re-traumatization by taking control and agency further away from a survivor.

Our job is about taking cues from survivors, which can be challenging when we feel we have something useful to offer. I am reminded of a very powerful story shared by Chris Mundell (2022) about a situation he dealt with while in an assistant dean of students role. I will capture the highlights here, but the full chapter is incredibly poignant and I would recommend a read. To summarize, Mundell received a call from a student alerting them to a situation of another student (pseudonym Jacob) who was actively threatening suicide. Mundell quickly convened the director of counseling and the director of safety and security and ultimately sent them to do a safety check on Jacob and assess what further supports he may need. Given the escalating situation and the reality that Jacob might need hospitalization, Mundell decided to contact Jacob's parents. Yet, very quickly into the call with Jacob's father, Mundell realized he had made a mistake. What Mundell did not know was that Jacob's father had long subjected him to both physical and emotional abuse. Jacob's father got off the phone, beat the directors to Jacob's apartment, and physically attacked Jacob for his "softness." Mundell expressed feelings of dismay and shame in realizing his attempts to support and help a student resulted in a situation of severe harm. He reflected on the situation and what he took away from it in the following way:

> operating from a trauma-informed perspective means a shift away from the belief that practitioners must play the role of the "protector" who has all the right answers and who is charged with making decisions on behalf of distressed students. Instead, I have come to embrace the trauma-informed approach that calls for mutuality in decision-making and a constant focus on offering students voice and choice in decisions that could impact their well-being.
>
> (p. 24)

What are some examples of providing resources and support mindfully?

- Ask. It seems simple and yet it's easy to forget when we're feeling difficult charged energy when students have been harmed. Ask students what they need and what they want to have happen (and what they don't).
- Resources are often deployed reactively, but proactive work needs to happen too. Not only do we need to have effective resources and

supports in place, but we also need to talk about them and normalize them long before they may ever be needed by a student. Since shame can be a feature of many traumatic experiences, we want to work toward campus cultures where using resources is embraced rather than something only done in the shadows.

Supporting Students Practice #6: Holding Space for Growth, Resilience, and Recuperation

There is little doubt that trauma produces considerable challenges for those who are traumatized by their experiences. Much of the work we do in a trauma-informed system is attentive to that challenge and difficulty. Yet, our work cannot rest solely in supporting students through the hard parts; it also needs to be attentive to their capacities for recuperation, resilience, and growth, because these can also be features of traumatic experiences. As activist and writer Adrienne Maree Brown (2017) reminds, "Resilience is in our nature, and we recover from things we would be justified in giving up over, again and again" (p. 126).

There is a robust body of work exploring a phenomenon known as posttraumatic growth (PTG; Tedeschi et al., 2018). PTG is described as "positive psychological changes experienced as a result of the struggle with traumatic or highly challenging life circumstances" (Tedeschi et al., 2018, p. 3). In other words, alongside the challenges of trauma (and in direct relation to working through those struggles), there is the possibility of not just returning to a previous baseline, but experiencing growth after traumatic experiences. Research about PTG has indicated five key domains where growth after trauma occurs, including a greater appreciation of life, recognition of one's strength alongside one's vulnerability, identification of new opportunities, positive changes in relating with others, and spiritual change.

I see holding space for growth as well as recuperation as a powerful part of our work in student affairs to support students who have experienced trauma. By holding space for good things, we create possibilities for hope, and hope itself is a powerful experience. Our capacity to hold open space for growth and resilience and recuperation ensures we aren't only focused on what's not working after trauma.

While necessary, it's an incomplete picture of traumatic experience. I appreciate Ginwright's (2018) re-frame that reminds us that instead of asking "What's wrong with you?" or even "What happened to you?" after trauma, that we instead shift to approaching those who have experienced trauma through the frame of "What's right with you?" The latter, he explains, "views those exposed to trauma as agents in the creation of their own well-being rather than victims of traumatic events" (Ginwright, 2018, para. 12).

The potential for growth after trauma often comes through empathetic relationships and what Tedeschi et al. (2018) refer to as *expert companionship*, which includes people who can sit patiently and comfortably with survivors and listen to their stories over and over again as those individuals process through their experiences. Expert companions can be mental health professionals, but Tedeschi et al. indicate that more frequently individuals experience this kind of companionship from friends and family. This expert companionship is a key piece of the potential of PTG. In essence, there is a tremendous power in being able to sit and listen and ask good questions in holding space for growth and resilience.

The potential of good things from trauma does not diminish the challenges. Yet, holding both at the same time offers a more complex and complete picture than either can do on their own. That complexity mirrors what I've learned from student survivors over the years who share versions of the story that as much as they have been challenged by trauma they have also learned things they can't imagine not knowing now. One of my participants, Aria, captured that both/and in the following way:

> I do think there's a lot that can be learned from my experience. I see it now as a source of power. I mean don't get me wrong, it still hurts like heck. It's still hard to talk about. It still really screws me up some days that some of this stuff happened, but being a mentee and having my mentors . . . has really shifted my ability to conceptualize the possibility of what it can all mean.

What are some examples of holding space for growth, resilience, and recuperation?

- Open up possibilities for survivors to reconnect with the fullness of their human experience, including laughter, awe, fun, joy, and meaning. We can create space for these elements in conversations we have with student survivors, experiences we generate, or opportunities that we connect survivors with.
- Remind ourselves in our work with student survivors that they are more than their trauma. Leave space in our work with survivors for asset-based explorations, such as: What are you proud of? What's working for you right now? What dreams and aspirations do you have? What brings you joy?

Complexities of Supporting Students Survivors

Many of us arrive to student affairs work with a desire to support students. That said, our student-centered motivations don't make the work easier. In relation to working with students who have experienced trauma, there are several complications that can make the work more challenging and are worth having on our radars. In the sections below, I want to name some of these complications so that we're aware of the challenges we may face as we engage in trauma-informed work with students. These realities make the landscape more challenging, but being able to name these difficulties as they arise can sometimes help. At the very least, we're aware of what we're confronting.

Difficult-to-Hear, Difficult-to-Sit-With

Trauma is hard for those enduring it. It can also be difficult for the people around survivors. Indeed, it's tempting to resist hearing about trauma, because these stories amplify our own vulnerabilities in the world—if this can happen to someone else, it can happen to us (Okello & Shalka, 2022). When we're learning about trauma of those we know well and care about, the impact hits us in terms of our own vulnerability, but also in terms of the difficulty of knowing that those we love have been harmed.

The realities of trauma being difficult-to-hear and difficult-to-sit-with mean that, yes, we instinctively resist learning about trauma, but also that when we do learn about it, there is a psychological and physical impact. We carry these stories with us to varying degrees. Many student affairs practitioners talk about challenges leaving their work at work, which can be amplified for live-in student affairs practitioners with no clear boundaries between work and home. This is even more complicated when the work involves exposure to trauma. Sometimes we can prepare ourselves for what that may be like, but I'm not sure that we can ever fully prepare ourselves for the ways the experiences of certain students will hit us deeply and stay with us in ways that can at times feel overwhelming and even haunting. There are strategies to help us work through these difficulties as I've discussed in the previous chapter, but we have to maintain an awareness that trauma in the lives of students we care about is inevitably difficult to hold and carry.

Personal Triggers

Earlier in this chapter, I discussed providing thoughtful referrals and making sure we're not just referring students along without first understanding why we are doing so. I also offered an important example of when we really may not be the best person to support a student and do need to refer them to someone else, which is when our own personal trauma history is being triggered.

Triggering is when something that we experience (whether it's something we hear, see, smell, etc.) reminds our body of a previous trauma, and it's like we're right back to that original state of fear and anxiety in our bodies. Student affairs professionals aren't immune from their own triggering experiences just because of their status as employees or leaders. Indeed, none of us have that luxury. But, there is a complicating factor for student affairs educators who may be interacting with others' traumas that ultimately trigger them to their own. Many student affairs professionals may feel caught in these kinds of situations, because on the one hand they want to be able to support students, while on the other hand doing so may come at a tremendous personal cost if it's possible at all. Defining boundaries of when to help and when to let students know we're not the person that is able to do so can be complicated for many reasons. These are, however, moments in which we need to be aware of creating the kinds of boundaries that help to preserve our own wellness while ensuring students are supported in other ways. Even in writing that, I know it's easier said than done in many situations for professionals who are often in the work for students, which is precisely why I name this as a complicating factor of trauma-informed student affairs practice.

Mandatory Reporting

Mandatory reporting is a complicated component of our work in colleges and universities. Both I and others (e.g., Freyd, 2016; Gómez, 2021; Holland et al., 2021) are critical of expansive mandatory reporting policies for sexual violence because they have the capacity to create further harm and traumatization. These are institutionalized forms of forced disclosure that when practiced expansively take agency and control away from survivors, who in college are by and large adults.

Although mandatory reporting policies are beyond the scope of this section, I want to highlight some important considerations in our work in relation to mandatory reporting policies. First, it is imperative that if and when we are a mandatory reporter on a campus we make that very clear to students who may want to self-disclose sexual violence to us, their own, or someone else's. The consequences of not doing that in advance only to have a student disclose sexual violence that we are forced to report with or without their consent can be devastating and re-traumatizing to a survivor. Second, part of our work in relation to mandatory reporting policies must be that of activism against expansiveness because of the harm that it creates. Freyd (2016) and Holland et al. (2021) are among those who have made calls for *mandatory supporting* rather than mandatory reporting policies. Working to nudge institutions and policymakers to blanket support rather than blanket reporting is something that I wholeheartedly endorse.

Institutional Betrayal

Dr. Jennifer Freyd is a researcher who is a pioneer in the field of trauma psychology and sexual violence. Her work has expanded our understanding of trauma, particularly in the aftermath of sexual violence, in profound ways. One of the concepts that she is known for developing is that of *institutional betrayal*. Freyd's theory of institutional betrayal accounts for "institutional action and inaction that exacerbate the impact of traumatic experiences" (Smith & Freyd, 2014, p. 577). In other words, institutional betrayal is harm inflicted by institutions when they either act (or fail to act) in ways that harm those who have already experienced trauma. Institutional betrayal makes trauma worse, as it represents an institution that should have done more to prevent harm and did not.

Institutional betrayal is a term that has a lot of applicability in institutions of higher education and I think many of us can likely conjure up examples that we have witnessed of this kind of harm that our institutions inflict on members of our campus communities whether students, staff, or faculty. I introduce the concept of institutional betrayal in this section because it might help bring language to a complication of supporting students through trauma that is otherwise difficult to put our fingers on. What can amplify the difficulty of supporting students through trauma is when we end up caught in the middle of a situation of being an institutional actor of an institution we know is causing harm to the student. These are situations that can be incredibly difficult to be entangled within, because there can be a sense of outrage and anger at the same time there are feelings of hopelessness and powerlessness that we can change these realities for students or ourselves. I will discuss institutional betrayal in further depth in Chapter 7.

Mattering

April was a participant in my previous research who endured an unimaginable trauma during college when she received a call from home letting her know that her mother had been murdered. What April went through was horrific in countless ways. I find it hard to do justice to all that she had to confront, and, yet, she found ways through the horrors and was able to persist as a college student, as many trauma survivors ultimately do. Something that was loud and clear in my conversations with April was the tremendous support system she had around her including friends, family of friends, and administrators at her school. Truly, if there is an example of student affairs administrators doing all the right things in terms of effectively supporting a student through trauma, the professionals with whom April interacted are the ultimate exemplars. As I shared in an earlier chapter, their collective work included examples like overriding a campus policy of no pets in residential housing so that April could have the comfort of bringing her family pet to school. It included examples like having a counselor present when April was taken to receive a call from the police officer calling to let her know what happened. It included high-level administrators checking in on her, coordinating needs with professors, and inviting April and her boyfriend for dinners with them. There are numerous other examples I could offer, but the clear message was that students really mattered at April's school and the way so many administrators and faculty held April as a human whom they cared about long after the immediate trauma was indicative of that.

There are tangible and tactical pieces to why effective support from student affairs educators can make such a difference in the wake of trauma. For example, student affairs professionals can provide resources and information that offer students pathways through their healing journeys. As previously mentioned, however, resources are the bare minimum. There's an even more critical ingredient that makes a difference after trauma and it comes down to something rather simple—mattering to others. Resources play a role in maneuvering through trauma, but what really seems to make the difference between surviving and thriving for survivors is that they very tangibly and specifically matter to someone. They matter to someone who is willing to walk alongside them through very difficult journeys. This mattering to someone is what helps survivors to recognize themselves as connected and human, which is significant because trauma can have dehumanizing effects and pull survivors away from the social order (van der Kolk, 2014).

In some of my recent research, I've learned that a sense of belonging may be compromised for those who suffer from PTSD (Shalka & Leal, 2022). Some elements that contribute to that diminished sense of belonging include things like the ways in which campus environments can feel unsafe after trauma (Shalka, 2021; Shalka & Leal, 2022). Additional intangibles that contribute to compromised belonging after trauma include the ways in which the world feels so different after trauma and those around a survivor who have not experienced the trauma may not know how to reach survivors in their new realities (Shalka, 2019b, 2021). This is where mattering to others is so consequential—survivors of trauma need to know that they matter to others and people care, even when those people may not know exactly how to make the trauma go away or what to say to make things feel better. Survivors aren't expecting magic wands. What they often need are simple acts of being acknowledged as whole and human—mattering to someone.

On a personal note, like April, I too was able to not just survive but thrive after trauma because of student affairs administrators and faculty who helped me know that I mattered to them. That's not to be taken lightly, because it's something that concerned me. I remember talking with friends about my fear that surviving the fire might be the most significant thing I would do in my life. In other words, I was worried I had lost my humanity and meaning and would be reduced forever to just that moment of survival. It was the collection of small gestures from those around me that reminded me of my worth as a person deserving of love and support.

How small? As small as an email. To offer just one example, I remember finally being back home in Canada and out of the hospital after a lengthy hospitalization following the fire in France. I was at my aunt's house and logging into my college email for the first time when I came across one from Professor Koop, one of my history professors. His email had been sent many weeks before, while I was still in the hospital. I remember the email began with him saying that if I was getting this he really should have tried an email much sooner, but he imagined I wouldn't be reading email for a long time. Instead, he had initially tried to get a physical letter to me via the dean's office to send to France, but that hadn't proved successful so he resorted to email. I remember exactly where I sat while reading that email. I remember exactly how it made me feel. I pictured Professor Koop using all these different strategies at his disposal just to reach me and to let me know that I mattered to him. In addition to being a professor, he was also a pastor, so we would ultimately have many good, deep conversations about my experiences in France in the years that followed, but what was important and started it all was just that simple email and effort to reach me and to let me know that I mattered to him. I needed that so much more than I'll ever be able to communicate. I needed that sense of mattering to others after trauma very deeply, and I have witnessed that same need among the many college student survivors of trauma that I have spoken to over the years. Never underestimate how powerful the simplest of gestures can be in the important work we all can do as educators to help student survivors of trauma know that they matter to us. Indeed, that is some of the most important work we can do as trauma-informed student affairs professionals.

Conclusion

In this chapter, I outlined six specific practices we can lean on in supporting college students through trauma, including nurturing relationships; being present; addressing issues of safety and control; attending to the complications of disclosure; providing resources and support mindfully; and holding space for growth, resilience, and recuperation. There are many things and resources we can offer survivors, yet very simply some of our most important work always comes back to ways of being outlined in the previous chapter and how we can create space to listen to and be with survivors who are seeking that kind of support. The work ultimately is profoundly relational and human-centered. In the next chapter, I'll extend the focus beyond support of students primarily impacted by trauma to look at student leaders and paraprofessionals (who may also be doing supporting work), and what they may need from us.

References

Brown, A. M. (2017). *Emergent strategy: Shaping change, changing worlds.* AK Press.

Erikson, K. (1995). Notes on trauma and community. In C. Caruth (Ed.), *Trauma: Explorations in memory* (pp. 183–199). Johns Hopkins University Press.

Freyd, J. J. (2016, December 1). Required supporting instead of required reporting: Responding well to disclosures of campus sexual violence. *HuffPost.* https://www.huffpost.com/entry/required-supporting-instead-of-required-reporting-responding_b_5831d0d1e4b0d28e552150c3

Ginwright, S. (2018, May 31). The future of healing: Shifting from trauma informed care to healing centered engagement. *Medium.* https://ginwright.medium.com/the-future-of-healing-shifting-from-trauma-informed-care-to-healing-centered-engagement-634f557ce69c

Gómez, J. M. (2021, June 8). *Reforming title IX: Evidence of harm of universal mandated reporting for marginalized survivors of campus sexual violence.* https://titleixdoelivehearingsgomez2021.blogspot.com/2021/06/reforming-title-ix-evidence-of-harm-of.html

Holland, K. J., Hutchison, E. Q., Ahrens, C., & Torres, M. G. (2021). Reporting is not supporting: Why mandatory supporting, not mandatory reporting, must guide university sexual misconduct policies. *Proceedings of the National Academy of Sciences of the United States of America, 118*(52). https://doi.org/10.1073/pnas.2116515118

Mundell, C. (2022). Doing no harm: One practitioner's journey towards trauma-informed practice. In T. R. Shalka & W. K. Okello (Eds.), *Trauma-informed practice in student affairs: Multidimensional considerations for care, healing, and wellbeing* (New Directions for Student Services, Vol. 177, pp. 17–25). Wiley. https://doi.org/10.1002/ss.20411

Okello, W. K., & Shalka, T. R. (2022). Introduction to trauma-informed practice in student affairs. In T. R. Shalka & W. K. Okello (Eds.), *Trauma-informed practice in student affairs: Multidimensional considerations for care, healing, and wellbeing* (New Directions for Student Services, Vol. 177, pp. 7–15). Wiley. https://doi.org/10.1002/ss.20410

Perry, B. D., & Winfrey, O. (2021). *What happened to you? Conversations on trauma, resilience, and healing.* Flatiron Books.

Remen, R. N. (2006). *Kitchen table wisdom: Stories that heal* (10th anniversary ed.). Riverhead Books.

Shalka, T. R. (2019a). Navigating the complex space of supporting student survivors of trauma. In P. M. Magolda, M. B. Baxter Magolda, & R. Carducci (Eds.), *Contested issues in troubled times: Student affairs dialogues on equity, civility, and safety* (pp. 221–232). Stylus.

Shalka, T. R. (2019b). Trauma and the interpersonal landscape: Developmental tasks of the relational self identity site. *Journal of College Student Development, 60*(1), 35–51. https://doi.org/10.1353/csd.2019.0002

Shalka, T. R. (2021). Traversing the shadow space: Experiences of spatiality after college student trauma. *The Review of Higher Education, 45*(1), 93–116. https://doi.org/10.1353/rhe.0.0176

Shalka, T. R. (2022). Nurturing a trauma-informed student affairs division. *About Campus, 27*(2), 18–25. https://doi.org/10.1177/10864822221100253

Shalka, T. R., & Leal, C. C. (2022). Sense of belonging for college students with PTSD: The role of safety, stigma, and campus climate. *Journal of American College Health, 70*(3), 698–705. https://doi.org/10.1080/07448481.2020.1762608

Smith, C. P., & Freyd, J. J. (2014). Institutional betrayal. *American Psychologist, 69*(6), 575–587. https://doi.org/10.1037/a0037564

Tedeschi, R. G., Shakespeare-Finch, J., Taku, K., & Calhoun, L. G. (2018). *Posttraumatic growth: Theory, research, and applications*. Routledge.

van der Kolk, B. A. (2014). *The body keeps the score: Brain, mind, and body in the healing of trauma*. Viking.

Venet, A. S. (2021). *Equity-centered trauma-informed education*. W. W. Norton & Company.

6

SUPPORTING STUDENT LEADERS WHO CARE FOR OTHERS

There's something about that Spider-Man quote, "With great power, comes great responsibility" (Raimi, 2002) that can conjure up some deeper sense of ethics and responsibility to others. It's one I've heard many people use in ways that are exactly that—oriented toward a recognition that we're interconnected and have responsibilities to one another in that interconnectivity. I've also heard that phrase used to invoke self-righteousness and martyrdom. In the context of the current chapter, I've heard that phrase used (explicitly or implicitly) to narrate how many people view the role of student leaders and peer educators on our campuses and the need to hold them to a higher standard.

In the context of trauma, I see some problems with that higher standard construction. Many student leaders and peer educators may be exposed to trauma in their roles, in addition to the trauma they may already carry with them. Given this, the higher standard construction can miss the nuance of what support student leaders may need through their work with the trauma of others and/or processing their own. In this chapter, I'll explore how we've come to conceptualize paraprofessionals and student leaders on many of our campuses and the implications of those framings in relation to trauma exposure. I'll also offer some tangible recommendations for how to shape our work with student leaders through a trauma-informed lens so that we can more effectively support them through their own potential encounters with trauma, whether that of others or their own.

Conceptualizing the Role of Student Leaders and Peer Educators/Paraprofessionals

Ender and Kay (2001, as cited in Shook & Keup, 2012, p. 6), define peer leaders as "students who have been selected and trained to offer educational services to their peers [that] are intentionally designed to assist in the adjustment, satisfaction, and persistence of students toward attainment of their educational goals." That definition certainly captures the umbrella of roles like orientation leaders (OLs), resident assistants (RAs), student conduct assistants, peer advisors, peer health educators, and tutors. These types of roles may be carefully designed and supervised by student affairs professionals (or other administrators or faculty on a campus). In the context of this chapter, I am discussing what Ender and Kay (2001) name as a peer leader role (one that may be considered a paraprofessional role) alongside other significant student leader positions on a campus such as those of leaders of student organizations whose roles are perhaps shaped more indirectly by the intentional advising of student affairs educators. I want us to think about all student leaders that we have significant touchpoints with, as opposed to just those who we select through hiring processes.

Regardless of paraprofessional or student leader broadly conceived, these collective roles often mean that the students who embody them find themselves in interesting in-between spaces. There are many research-documented benefits to that in-between (Shook & Keup, 2012) that we as student affairs educators often tout, including possibilities for transformational learning and development. I know that to be personally true. When I think back on my college experience, there were numerous transformational experiences, but some of the most profound were those in which I was a peer leader. I changed in ways that continue to be part of the undercurrent of who I am to this day because of my roles as a leader in my sorority and an RA. I learned to navigate really complex situations with my peers that I look back on now and can't believe I was navigating as a 21-year-old. Although there was certainly growth and good things for me through those roles, there were also things I was navigating and expectations on me as a student leader that in other respects I should not have been handling or responsible for and I think that's true for many student leaders on numerous campuses.

Peer leaders and student paraprofessionals are often on the front lines of many challenging situations. Ganser and Kennedy (2012) highlight how resident assistants (RAs) are frequently not just expected to be part of crisis management but are, in practice (because of the live-in status of their roles), often the very first to respond to crises before even medical assistance or police or others are able to arrive. The exact same scenario could be true for many other student leaders such as those living in their sorority or fraternity. That's not new information to those of us who work in student affairs, but it's worth pausing to consider what that means practically for the RAs and other student leaders involved in very difficult and often traumatic situations to which they are exposed.

RAs are an easy place for us to see the potential for trauma exposure in the context of paraprofessional or peer leader roles, but it's equally important we're attentive to the potential for all student leaders to be exposed to trauma during their responsibilities. Sometimes, the unexpected nature of how trauma can arise in roles that may not explicitly include crisis management as part of the job may make it potentially more jarring for students. I learned of one such example in some of my recent research from a participant, Margot. She was working in the call center for her campus development office and her specific role was to call parents to ask for donations to the university. She characterized the role as generally enjoyable, and that even if parents didn't want to donate additional money to the school, they were pleasant and wanting to learn more about her experience as a student. However, one day Margot was on the phone with a parent who got verbally aggressive with her as he stated in no uncertain terms he had no interest in donating money to the school. As the conversation progressed, the father revealed his daughter had been sexually assaulted at the institution and started yelling at Margot, blaming her by association for the institution's lack of action. The experience was difficult for Margot for a variety of reasons, but critically because she too had been sexually assaulted at the same university. That call brought up many strong feelings and thoughts for Margot, including her being upset that the father had revealed this to her, because she felt it compromised his daughter's privacy since Margot could have figured out who it was. This was a triggering moment for Margot in part because her own sexual assault experience had been shared in ways beyond her control at the institution. Additionally, there was really no space for Margot to process that phone call or step away from her assigned job—she had to go right onto the next call. I had the sense that she also didn't have the opportunity or didn't perceive she had the opportunity to process the call with a supervisor later. So maybe this is exactly the kind of example that demonstrates missed opportunities to support students through trauma exposure when we assume only certain kinds of student leader roles will mean trauma exposure. Exposure can happen in myriad places—on phone calls like Margot's experience, via an assignment that a student writing tutor or teaching assistant reads, or many other examples we can brainstorm.

The Dangers of the Superhuman Construction in Relation to Trauma

I started my student affairs career working in residential life, so it's the source of many reflections when I consider what it means to effectively support and train peer leaders in the context of the trauma they may be exposed to in their roles. I recall many a residential life professional staff meeting discussing various concerns about members of our RA staff, usually in relation to behavior that the department deemed problematic. I specifically remember one meeting where a colleague and I seemed to be the minority opinion advocating on behalf of an RA that the department felt we needed to terminate because of their behavior. I don't remember the details of the situation, but I remember that what the colleague and I kept saying in different language was some version of "But they are a student too. Why aren't they allowed to just have a student experience that other students are having?" And the collective response from the department was, "Because they are an RA. They're held to a higher standard." The higher standard argument was a familiar one to me. It's the same message I heard myself as an undergraduate RA. It was drilled into us that we were not like the other students, because there were higher expectations on us by virtue of our roles.

I find that higher standard construction problematic. There were elements that felt somewhat intoxicating to me as a student—how amazing it felt to be seen and held as somehow exceptional on this campus of exceptional people. Yet, perhaps that intoxicating feeling should have been a red flag. These days, I see several problems with that construction including how it creates a superhuman expectation of peer leaders that is inherently fraught because at the end of the day they are not superhuman—they are *human* and *students*.

Am I advocating that we don't hold student leaders to high standards? Not in the slightest. I'm advocating that we have expectations in balance with the realities of where student leaders are at in their lives, which includes being first and foremost in college to be students. Although we often rely on them because of their amazingness, they're also not full-time professionals, nor impermeable superheroes who walk through life unscathed.

Related to trauma, the higher standard construction is problematic for at least a couple of reasons. First, higher standard rhetoric can lead to isolating conditions as those expectations may inadvertently mean student leaders are less and less capable of participating in campus life and even pre-existing relationships with other students in the same ways that their peers do. Isolation is of deep concern to me, because it's a status that can amplify an individual's preexisting experiences of trauma or secondary trauma as well as reduce the likelihood that a student leader is able to connect with others for support as they're exposed to new trauma. Isolation is a status we don't talk enough about in relation to trauma but is frequently a condition that those who have been exposed find themselves feeling in the aftermath of trauma. Second, the higher standard narrative and corresponding implicit messages of needing to be superhuman can inadvertently signal to student leaders who are confronting trauma in their roles that there is something wrong with them if they feel human emotions and reactions to what they witness. The reality, of course, is that trauma is deeply difficult and deeply humanizing and we need student leaders who are trained to know that it's ok to not feel ok in the face of these experiences.

Sometimes the superhuman expectations we place on student leaders arrive incidentally or at the very least unintentionally. Sometimes, it's because we exist in systems that are already overstrained and constrained. The overstrain can happen because units may not have enough resources to do the jobs expected of them, and sometimes work is pushed on students because we can't do it all ourselves. The constraints frequently arrive because of external factors (sometimes legal or otherwise) that make it difficult for institutional actors to make decisions that protect those "on the ground." These conditions of overstrain or constraint can contribute to putting student leaders into harmful situations that demand a superhuman.

Let me share a concrete example to illustrate this point from my time as a residential life professional supervising an RA staff. One of the residents in our building was really struggling and periodically in states of expressing active suicide ideation. The situation was exceedingly complicated, but the result for my RA who had this student living on their floor was excruciating. There are numerous details to the story that I am omitting here for the sake of brevity, but the institutional message I kept getting was that we could not remove the student from the residence hall.

The impact on my RA was horrific. He was in my office multiple times a day or contacting me by email or phone at other times because he was beside himself. The institution wasn't able to change the student's living situation and was asking that the RA keep an eye on the resident. That expectation had my RA in a state of barely sleeping and constantly preoccupied with the resident's safety, because the RA (understandably) knew he couldn't live with himself if something happened on his floor. When I heard he was going to the resident's door at night and just standing there to listen and make sure he could still hear the resident breathing, I knew we were far past reasonable expectations on this RA. Yet, our leadership and the institution had nothing else to offer. Yes, they were available to provide counseling for the RA and I was there to support him and keep trying to advocate for changes, but none of us were the ones there with that RA living on that floor constantly on edge that something could happen.

I didn't have the language or understanding I have now to recognize the trauma dimensions of what was happening for my RA. Perhaps if I had, I could have been advocating in different ways to support the well-being of my RA in what I realize now was a very complicated legal and ethical situation for the institution. I'm not convinced in these situations that we've done enough to prepare and train ourselves to adequately support student leaders who are exposed to trauma. I certainly wasn't prepared enough as a 20-something, a year or two out of my master's program, and I came in with some additional skills relative to many because of my own background and training.

We can't remove trauma exposure from the lives of student leaders and paraprofessionals, nor do I see that as our goal. That said, there's more work to do in placing the potential for trauma exposure forefront on our radars as we prepare to train and work with student leaders and peer educators. Below, I will offer some ideas about how to move forward in this endeavor.

Recommendations for Training and Supporting Student Leaders Through a Trauma Lens

Effective training and support of student leaders who may be exposed to trauma come first by establishing some edges and boundaries for their roles. That boundary work includes us clearly conceptualizing the edges of our expectations of students in these roles. Then, we must make sure we provide adequate supports to help students stay within those boundaries. In other words, we need to envision expectations that minimize harm to student leaders (e.g., by reducing superhuman constructions), while recognizing they will still encounter trauma and thus ensuring they're prepared to do so when it happens. In the sections that follow I discuss what student leaders need to know about trauma, how to prepare them for trauma exposure, and then how to support student leaders who have encountered that exposure.

Teaching About Trauma

A persistent theme in this book is the importance of education about trauma as foundational to trauma-informed work. The more people on a college campus who understand trajectories of trauma, the better it is for those who encounter trauma, because there will be a network of other people who potentially understand what those survivors may be experiencing. I can think of no better group on a college campus to be prepared with this kind of knowledge than student leaders and paraprofessionals because of the immense reach they have on a campus and their frequent touchpoints with peers. Not only are peer leaders an important component of information dissemination on a campus (Shook & Keup, 2012), but they are the network of people who are there with peers at 2 am when those of us who are staff and faculty aren't. Student leaders may well be the most likely individuals on a campus to encounter the trauma of their peers. Thus, educating peer leaders about trauma means they can both draw on and share that knowledge around a campus and bolster collective understandings of trauma.

Teaching student leaders about trauma includes the following: (a) educating about how trauma impacts those who experience it and (b) preparing them for their own personal responses to secondary trauma exposure (which I'll discuss in a separate section below). The former prepares student leaders to recognize the possibility of traumatization in their peers and perhaps offer better support to those peers along the way. That, alone, could make such a difference from the experience one of my participants, Liv, articulated in feeling she had lived beyond the collective experience of her peer group after her experience navigating the suicide of her close friend from home. The more students who understand the nature of trauma on a college campus, the less likely students like Liv might be to struggle in isolation without peers who understand.

There are many places to infuse trauma education for student leaders. It's helpful to think about meeting needs based on what student leaders may be exposed to, while also being attentive to presenting information during periods when student leaders can metabolize it. For example, it might be great to do trauma education during RA or OL training or during a retreat with student organization leaders. We could also make the argument that RA/OL training weeks are already overwhelming in ways that student leaders may not have the mental or emotional space to internalize or make meaning of all they need to regarding trauma. We might consider introducing trauma education during a training week, but revisit it later, cognizant of sequencing when it may be most relevant. For example, perhaps we teach about trauma and even secondary traumatic stress during an RA summer training week, but we revisit the secondary traumatic stress topic with RAs during the semester when exposure to residents' traumas may be occurring for RAs. Opportunities to introduce topics across time and sometimes even with repetition tend to work better than one-time sessions. The over-time model allows us to tailor to specific needs and contexts whether we think about that in relation to a certain point in time during the semester or the likelihood of exposure to different things based on the student leader's role. As we consider how to find multiple touchpoints in educating student leaders about trauma, some of those touchpoints may occur in more traditional training or workshop formats, while others might be in more informal ways like 1:1 conversations with students or resources that we share.

Whether formal or informal mechanisms of trauma education, we must be attentive to the reality that in any group we're a part of there will inevitably be numerous people who are survivors of trauma. That means we proceed mindfully with a trauma-informed approach, in which we are attentive to creating safety, predictability, and working to minimize the potential for re-traumatization or further harm. This can happen in very small ways, such as providing content warnings in advance to student leaders about what information is to be shared, providing choices for how students engage with the content (including choosing not to), and proactively working to strengthen relationships and connections within groups to provide additional possibilities of safety in discussing difficult topics.

Preparing Student Leaders for Working With Trauma Survivors

Preparing student leaders to work with those who have experienced trauma begins with some of that boundary and edge work I mentioned at the start of the chapter. It's important to articulate to student leaders that they are not therapists, nor do we expect them to be. Ultimately, we're trying to prepare student leaders to be good supports for peers who have experienced trauma to the extent that those student leaders can while remaining well themselves. We aren't asking them to solve all problems the survivor may be confronting or to become their de facto counselor, which can contribute to significant stress and overwhelm for student leaders.

Yet, this can be a difficult balance for peer leaders to achieve because of their proximity to peers (sometimes even living in the same place). As a recent study of RAs and trauma exposure found, RAs articulated very clearly an understanding that they were not counselors, yet they still found themselves in challenging roles listening to and helping residents process traumatic situations that perhaps paralleled the emotional toll of being a counselor without all the skills to do so (Crivello, 2020). Thus, our support in helping student leaders to identify the edges of what their support could or should look like is important. Student leaders may well need us to guide them through that exploration by asking them good reflective questions and/or helping them recognize when they are reacting in ways that exceed the edges of their roles and may ultimately be personally harmful.

Some of this support can be achieved by helping student leaders to consider what boundaries they need in their work. Something I think about a lot in this respect is: How do we help student leaders develop sufficient self-awareness, confidence, and self-advocacy skills to be able to (a) recognize personal limits of what they're able to confront and what they aren't and (b) articulate that to others? This is where there can be challenges in climates of "higher standards" because these cultures may inadvertently send messages that it's a peer leader's job to be able to handle any kind of crisis.

Whether I'm working with administrators or faculty or students about supporting others through trauma, I'm careful to mention the importance of self-work and being clear on what we're able to do and not able to do. Sometimes we're not the best person to support someone else when their experience of trauma is triggering our own, for example. Taking the time to help student leaders pause and define their personal boundaries is important, as is helping them to identify in advance some of the information that they could rely on to alert them when they are crossing a boundary. In the moment, it's easy to be caught up in problem-solving and lose sight of boundaries. Imagine, though, that we've helped a peer leader reflect in advance on how embodied information may tell them something about their boundaries with trauma. For example, that when they feel the surge of an anxiety response erupting that it may be their body's way of telling them they need to pause and assess. That can make a huge difference.

We need to create more structures for pause and reflection for our peer leaders, so they can rehearse in advance of these challenging situations. Higher education cultures often promote do-do-do, but we need to be more intentional about helping to both model and teach peer leaders to slow down, pause, and engage in reflection.

The next part of preparing student leaders for working with survivors is normalization. We explicitly name the reality that trauma exposure can be difficult and impact us in profound ways. It can be useful to discuss elements of secondary traumatic stress and the ways in which exposure to others' traumas can wear on us (see Chapter 4, for example, from van Dernoot Lipsky [2009] excellent book that outlines 16 warning signs of trauma exposure with negative impacts). Being aware of these possibilities allows student leaders to be able to identify their own experience when it happens and perhaps in that naming be more able to seek help and support.

I recently heard an interesting take about compassion fatigue and secondary trauma on an episode of Brené Brown's (2022) *Unlocking Us* podcast that I think is useful in helping student leaders to consider the edges of their boundaries in relation to the kind of support they do with students who have experienced trauma. What Brown shared in this podcast episode was the idea that there is a difference between an empathetic engagement with someone's trauma and a traumatic engagement with someone's trauma. In the latter, we're inserting ourselves into the storyline in ways that it makes it traumatic and real for us. Brown shared the example of being very upset after the Sandy Hook shootings and going through it in detail with her therapist, seemingly imagining every detail of what it would have been like and imagining herself experiencing it. Brown expressed that she was trying to feel what it was like in detail to empathize. Her therapist stopped her and prompted Brown to think about a workshop she had recently facilitated with survivors of sexual assault. The therapist asked Brown if she'd imagined every detail of those individuals' situations. Brown explained she hadn't or she wouldn't have been able to do her job. That is the difference—we're empathetic by holding space and sitting with others. We're not being empathetic when we're inserting ourselves into their stories to re-experience what they have experienced. In that case we're in fact creating harm and trauma for ourselves. Thus, part of the boundaries we can help students understand is in relation to that nuance of what it means to be empathetic while not inserting oneself into another's trauma.

Finally, in addition to the preparation work of reflecting on boundaries and normalizing trauma as difficult, it's also important to provide students with some skills for how to be in relation to trauma when they do encounter it. I have done some of this work in preparing students who work with me on my research by offering intentional de-briefing time about the trauma they are exposed to in addition to offering them tools such as journaling, visualization exercises, or the importance of being active in physically helping to move trauma out of our bodies (i.e., going for a walk, taking a shower).

A therapist of mine several years ago taught me a few wonderful exercises that I use to this day to help my body release the trauma of others. I use these when I am in data collection hearing others' traumas and I have taught these exercises to some of the students who work with me. Either could be good tools to pass along to student leaders to use after trauma exposure. What we're trying to achieve with these two exercises is helping our body to know what is ours to hold versus what is the trauma of others that we don't need to take on as our own. I offer these exercises below as options to consider, but there are many other such activities that can also be useful.

Exercise #1: Visualization for Releasing

Find a comfortable standing or sitting position. Begin by closing your eyes if that's comfortable to you or leaving them open with a soft gaze, not focusing on anything in particular. Take a few moments to focus on your breath. Next, imagine the trauma that you've heard and/or learned about from others within your body. For some, it might be helpful to feel sensations of that information in the body; for others, it might be helpful to imagine a visual representation of where and how that information is in the body; and for others, it might be helpful to imagine a sound that represents that information in the body. Then, begin to imagine all that trauma information (in terms of the feelings, the visualization, or the sound) as leaving your body out of your elbows or the bottoms of your feet.

Exercise #2: Visualization for Putting in a Box

Find a comfortable position (whether seated or lying down). Close your eyes if that's comfortable to you or leave them open with a soft gaze, not focusing on anything in particular. Begin by imagining a box. It can be any kind of box you want. The box is as big or as small as you need it to be. You can imagine decorating it by adding colors, bows, or whatever you want. Next, imagine the trauma that you've been exposed to or the emotions or memories related to it that might be challenging at various points. Take any and all of those things that might be feeling like too much or too much for right now, and invite them inside that lovely box that you've decorated. As you engage in this process, imagine and notice those thoughts going into the box without feeling you need to force them there. Then, imagine a room that feels safe and inviting with a shelf or closet where you can go and place that box. Then gently and mindfully imagine placing your box on that shelf with love, knowing that you can return to the box and go through its contents whenever you want, but you're also able to put it away when you need to, too.

Note: If visualization is something that feels a bit too abstract, another way to do this activity is in terms of using a physical box and then writing down some of those overwhelming thoughts or feelings on pieces of paper and putting them inside the box.

Creating Intentional and Effective Support for Student Leaders After Exposure to Trauma

In the aftermath of trauma, our work shifts from thinking about how to anticipate and prepare student leaders for trauma exposure, to working to help support them through the potential challenges that exposure can catalyze. In helping fields, one of the important protective factors against experiencing secondary traumatic stress is that of supervision (Northeastern University's Institute on Urban Health Research and Practice, n.d.). In the context of student leaders and paraprofessionals, this means we must be attentive to our role as supervisors and advisors in actively working to minimize the negative impacts student leaders may encounter in relation to trauma exposure.

This includes maintaining regular touchpoints with students, creating space for discussing trauma exposure if students would like to, and monitoring student leaders for signs of secondary traumatic stress. Below, I discuss some of the more specific ways we can work with student leaders who are in immediate distress after trauma exposure as well as some considerations for how to provide continued effective supports over time.

Immediate Distress: Psychological First Aid

Some trauma exposure for peer leaders and paraprofessionals will be upsetting enough that they will experience distress immediately following the exposure. For example, a fraternity president who finds a member who has attempted suicide is likely to be shaken by the experience and need support in the immediate aftermath. Certainly, some trauma exposures may require we connect peer leaders and paraprofessionals with formal mental health support. Whether a student ultimately needs that kind of support or not, there is also work we can do as student affairs professionals to support students and understand their needs.

One possible approach is psychological first aid (PFA), which is a model used to support individuals through distress after a crisis or trauma exposure (World Health Organization [WHO], 2013). Though "psychological" is in the title, you don't have to be a trained mental health professional to use it. PFA is an approach and framework that offers something tangible to lean on when we're supporting student leaders in the aftermath of trauma exposure. As with any of the approaches that I offer in this section, this is a suggestion and simply one possible approach. This is by no means the only way to offer support nor will it be the best approach in every situation. Additionally, while I will provide some basic overview of PFA below, I would encourage anyone interested in using it to seek out additional resources to learn about the nuances of the approach and how to implement it mindfully and appropriately.

PFA is an approach to listening and gaging needs, but importantly, it is not one that pressures a person to talk about their experience or analyze it (WHO, 2013). Listening is emphasized in PFA, but not to the point of pressured or formal debriefing. PFA is predicated on three key elements connected to better outcomes for those who have experienced a crisis. Specifically, individuals tend to do better if they: (a) feel safe, connected to others, calm, and hopeful; (b) have access to social, physical, and emotional support; and (c) regain a sense of control by being able to help themselves (WHO, 2013, p. 22). The steps of PFA contribute to bolstering these three components.

PFA is intended to be used in the aftermath of a crisis when individuals are still in distress (WHO, 2013). This could be immediately after an experience or even in the weeks after if distress is still present. There are four key components to engaging in PFA, including Prepare, Look, Listen, and Link.

In the *prepare* phase, helpers (in this case student affairs staff or faculty) familiarize themselves with basic details about the crisis, acquaint themselves with available supports and resources, and gage concerns about safety and security. During the prepare phase, helpers should be attentive to their own well-being and make sure they're taking time to prepare themselves emotionally and practically to engage with those in distress.

In the *look* phase, helpers engage in some basic assessment. First and foremost, helpers need to assess the environment for safety before engaging with others in PFA. Additionally, helpers pay attention to who may be in serious distress and what basic needs those impacted may have.

Helpers then *listen*. They intentionally approach those who are distressed and create space to simply listen to those individuals and their needs. During this phase, it's important that the helpers try to maintain a sense of calm and are aware of how their own presence can continue to communicate calm. Critically, listening is an invitation in this phase, but not a mandate. We're intentionally making space for those experiencing distress to share what they need or want to and check in about their needs, but we're not forcing that conversation.

Finally, in the *link* phase, helpers are attentive to connection. Based on what they may have learned through "looking" and "listening," helpers work to connect students in distress to useful resources and supports. Although informational resources or mental health supports may be obvious possibilities, the importance of connection is a critical part of healing in the wake of trauma and distress. Thus, this linking phase is also one where we consider how we can facilitate connecting students to community, family, friends, and the like that may be important as they process through trauma exposure.

Ongoing Support

In the days, weeks, and months that follow trauma exposure, student leaders may need a variety of different supports. Recall from earlier chapters that trauma is experienced subjectively—what is traumatic to one person may not be to another. The same is true of what might occur for student leaders exposed to others' traumas. In some situations, student leaders may not be impacted in any significant ways, while in other situations, student leaders may face significant distress. The suggestions below are some offerings in terms of what we *might* consider working with student leaders after they have been exposed to trauma—some of these strategies will be useful in certain contexts and not others. We ultimately need to rely on our professional judgment and assessment of the situation to better understand what individual students may need.

Practical Considerations

In the aftermath of trauma exposure, student leaders may need relatively straightforward supports, particularly in terms of helping them restore a sense of safety and balance. First, we must ensure student leaders feel safe. If their sense of safety is compromised by what they experienced, we work to resolve that situation. Examples might include needs for changed housing or distance from particular people. Second, it's useful to acknowledge what has happened. Sometimes, the temptation for institutions and institutional actors is to try to get back to "normal" and act as if nothing has happened. That reflex can be difficult for those exposed to trauma, because for them things do not feel normal, nor do they just forget what happened. It seems very simple, but creating space either in 1:1 conversations, within groups, or in communications to acknowledge that something difficult has happened is an important component of effective support. Finally, we can consider structural mechanisms that provide student leaders with the kind of support they need to re-establish equilibrium. That might mean helping to alleviate or lessening workloads for paraprofessionals, while for some students it might mean wanting to be involved in different kinds of projects to stay busy while they process what has happened at a pace that feels good to them. Structural supports might also mean creating purposeful mechanisms that normalize having space to process trauma exposure. In relation to RAs and the potential for secondary traumatic stress, Sorensen (2018) suggests regular group processing sessions hosted in collaboration with counselors throughout the semester that RAs can opt into and discuss any challenging or traumatic situations they've dealt with during the semester.

Peer Mentorship

In research about RAs and trauma exposure, Crivello (2020) discusses how veteran RAs rely on previous experiences supporting students through trauma to inform subsequent experiences. This finding has some implications for the importance of peer mentorship in relation to trauma exposure for student leaders. Creating spaces where peer leaders can share about the trauma exposure they have experienced in the past creates numerous important conditions. First, this type of sharing might help newer leaders to gain valuable insights from more experienced leaders in relation to dealing with trauma exposure. Second, and perhaps even more importantly, it helps to normalize the experience in ways that newer student leaders can hear from experienced leaders about their own struggles. This type of sharing can help new leaders recognize that they aren't alone in feeling difficult emotions in relation to what they're exposed to and perhaps be that much more willing to reach out for support as needed when they recognize others have to as well.

Creating Space for Humor and Play

van der Kolk (2014) notes the ways in which trauma can rob individuals of a sense of spontaneity, because the nervous system after trauma becomes consumed with navigating feelings of chaos and unsafety.

Thus, part of long-term support after trauma exposure is that of creating opportunities for enjoyment and spontaneity again. Trauma is heavy, and there are many difficult emotions that come with confronting it. Yet, we can find ways to balance that heaviness out with lightness, too. Crivello (2020) notes how RAs often use humor as a coping mechanism after trauma exposure, and that's a finding I think we can lean more into. As supervisors or advisors working with student leaders who have had exposure to trauma through their roles, there is certainly a place and time for us to create space for processing that trauma. However, there is equally a need for us to create space for humor, play, and creativity. Playing a game in a staff meeting or doing a creative project in a workshop with student leaders or finding time in a 1:1 to laugh about a shared experience can go a long way to help reconnect student leaders with the fullness of their human experience rather than sitting solely in and with the pain of trauma exclusively.

Conclusion

For many of us in student affairs, our interactions with student leaders are among the most rewarding parts of our work. They are amazing and capable students who make so many things possible on the college campuses of which they're a part. Unfortunately, that also means they are among those most likely to encounter the trauma of peers and find themselves in vulnerable positions as a result. In this chapter, I discussed some of the things we need to keep an eye on connected to that reality, including ways to minimize superhuman constructions of peer leaders and effectively preparing student leaders for the encounters they may have with trauma.

References

Brown, B. (Host). (2022, May 18). Atlas of the heart, audience Q&A, part 1 of 2. *Unlocking us* [Audio podcast episode]. https://brenebrown.com/podcast/atlas-of-the-heart-audience-qa-part-1-of-2/#transcript

Crivello, K. A. (2020). *The management of secondary trauma experiences for resident assistants in housing and residential life* (Publication No. 27993544) [Master's thesis, California State University]. ProQuest Dissertations Publishing.

Ender, S. C., & Kay, K. (2001). Peer leadership programs: A rationale and review of the literature. In S. L. Hamid (Ed.), *Peer leadership: A primer on program essentials*. (Monograph no. 32, National Resource Center for The First-Year Experience and Students in Transition). University of South Carolina.

Ganser, S. R., & Kennedy, T. L. (2012). Where it all began: Peer education and leadership in student services. In J. R. Keup (Ed.), *Peer leadership in higher education* (New Directions for Higher Education, Vol. 157, pp. 17–29). Wiley.

Northeastern University's Institute on Urban Health Research and Practice. (n.d.). *Guidelines for a vicarious trauma-informed organization: Supervision.* https://ovc.ojp.gov/sites/g/files/xyckuh226/files/media/document/sup_in_a_vt_informed_organization-508.pdf

Raimi, S. (Dir.). (2002). *Spider-Man* [Film]. Columbia Pictures; Marvel Enterprises; Laura Ziskin Productions.

Shook, J. L., & Keup, J. R. (2012). The benefits of peer leader programs: An overview from the literature. In J. R. Keup (Ed.), *Peer leadership in higher education* (New Directions for Higher Education, Vol. 157, pp. 5–16). Wiley.

Sorensen, E. A. (2018). *Situational stress factors and secondary traumatic stress among resident assistants* [Doctoral dissertation, Miami University]. OhioLINK. https://etd.ohiolink.edu/apexprod/rws_etd/send_file/send?accession=miami1532678812601448&disposition=inline

van der Kolk, B. A. (2014). *The body keeps the score: Brain, mind, and body in the healing of trauma*. Viking.

van Dernoot Lipsky, L. (2009). *Trauma stewardship: An everyday guide to caring for self while caring for others*. With C. Burk. Berrett-Koehler.

World Health Organization, War Trauma Foundation and World Vision International. (2013). *Psychological first aid: Facilitator's manual for orienting field workers*. WHO.

7

THE ORGANIZATIONAL END GOAL
EQUITY-FOCUSED SYSTEMS OF WELLNESS AND CARE

This seems a good time to review the crux of what we're trying to accomplish in trauma-informed practice. In its most basic form, trauma-informed practice is about taking knowledge and information about trauma and its trajectories and using that to guide our practice, policies, and interactions (Pope, 2022). As Venet (2021) names, this work must be engaged not just individually, but also structurally. In other words, many trauma-informed systems may get stuck in doing this work at the level of resources and support for individuals primarily impacted by trauma as opposed to working on systemic level concerns such as those in which we see how our organizations themselves may create trauma and harm.

Certainly, trauma-informed practice is about improving experiences for those primarily impacted by trauma. Yet, it's also about creating systems that are beneficial to all. Fundamentally, trauma-informed systems are those oriented toward healing and use equity, wellness, and care as guideposts alongside knowledge about trauma and its trajectories. Thus, the organizational end goal of trauma-informed practice is exactly that—creating wellness and care-centric systems. In doing this *both/and* work of being attentive to both individuals and systems, I think we're better able to live into the kind of deep healing that Adrienne Maree Brown (2017) speaks of in saying that "healing happens when a place of trauma or pain is given full attention, really listened to" (p. 34). It's a healing that comes from centering and listening to trauma and, in our higher education context, that kind of healing takes the attention of an entire campus community.

I like to do some thought exercises to imagine what it would look like and feel like to work or study in a truly trauma-informed organization (Venet, 2021). In short, it would be powerful. I was recently asked this question for an episode of Student Affairs NOW (Pope, 2022), and some of the descriptors that I mentioned about being in a trauma-informed environment include there being intentional pausing, space for grace, and for holding each other with care and humanity. *Sit with that for a moment. What does it feel like in your body to imagine being in that kind of environment?* For me, it feels really good. When I imagine that kind of environment, I feel like my muscles can relax and stop gripping so hard. My body can start to release stress or the pressure to move at frenetic paces. I can feel a sense of spaciousness and openness that comes right behind that. I can also feel little sparkles of joy as I imagine the ways I would be able to move through and exist within that kind of supportive and nurturing environment.

In that environment I imagine that I'm given the benefit of the doubt, and when I'm less than perfect or make mistakes or seem "off" that the people around me approach me with curiosity and care rather than judgment or condemnation. I also can feel an environment where I'm challenged beyond the edges of my own experiences and actively engaged in learning about the edges of others' experiences as we work collectively to envision and enact equity. In short, this vision of a trauma-informed environment would help me to feel safe, supported, challenged, and understood.

This is where we begin in this chapter—imagining the end goal of trauma-informed organizations as centered on wellness, care, and equity, while grounded in and informed by knowledge about trauma. In what follows, I will discuss some of the barriers to making this happen at a systems level in higher education. Then, I will pivot to talking about how we get there despite the barriers.

Organizational Barriers to Trauma-Informed Practices

There is certainly increased attention to trauma these days and trauma-informed practice exists as a topic in many organizations that many people would be interested in engaging in (at least in theory). Yet, there's a lot of organizational momentum and examples of status quos that work very much in opposition to the goals of trauma-informed policies and practices. I want to highlight four of these organizational barriers below, including institutional betrayal, trauma production, climates that are driven by risk management and litigation fear, and discomfort-resistant leadership.

Institutional Betrayal

As mentioned briefly in a previous chapter, Dr. Jennifer Freyd is a pioneer in the trauma psychology world who has brought several profound and useful concepts to advance our understandings of what happens to survivors of trauma (especially sexual violence in her work). One of the concepts that emerged from her decades of research is that of *institutional betrayal*. Institutional betrayal, as a reminder, is when an institution's actions or inactions "exacerbate the impact of traumatic experiences" (Smith & Freyd, 2014, p. 577). Smith and Freyd (2014) further elaborate that institutional betrayal is experienced when any individual within an organization experiences a violation of their trust and dependency in that organization. It's important to note that individuals don't have to have deep trust in their institutions to feel betrayed by them. For example, a racially minoritized student or staff member at a predominantly White institution (PWI) may have ample reasons to already distrust their organization, but trust and dependency are established by virtue of the fact that the student or staff member has a contract with that institution (for an education in the former case or for employment in the latter). Additionally, Smith and Freyd note that anytime an individual reaches out for help, there is an inherent trust that is opened up in seeking assistance or a solution and that trust can be violated when that need isn't met.

Although there are negative consequences for both individuals and institutions themselves when institutional betrayal is present, there are several reasons that organizations may continue to enact this kind of harm (Smith & Freyd, 2014). First, organizations may lack the language needed to name and describe the injury that is happening, which means that every time that harm occurs, it's almost like it's happening for the first time. In other words, names, labels, and language are needed to connect the dots of systemic patterns and provide common ways to realize that what is happening in one instance is an example of what happened in another. Second, organizations may have a strong internal (conscious or unconscious) tendency to "not know." Organizations may maintain a seeming unawareness of harm as an act of self-protection, because owning the reality of the micro or macro violences they may be creating may be an uncomfortable position to sit in. Finally, organizations may be seemingly resistant to change because they are acting out of their own traumatization. For an organization that is itself traumatized over time and the decision makers within it experience this reality, there can be many self-protective mechanisms in place to avoid additional overwhelm.

Actions and inactions in an organization that perpetuate institutional betrayal are at odds with what would be needed from a trauma-informed organization. Indeed, institutional betrayal creates several amplifications of traumatization and negative experiences for those who have survived trauma. For example, institutional betrayal increases the potential of posttraumatic stress symptoms in those who experience it (Smith & Freyd, 2013). Thus, we need to recognize institutional betrayal as a condition that works directly against efforts at trauma-informed practice, as it can create additional forms of trauma.

Trauma Production

A significant organizational barrier to trauma-informed practice is that of viewing trauma as something that happens "out there." By "out there" I mean that often institutions and institutional actors are reacting to trauma as if it's something that happens in the context of students' and employee's lives separate from the institution. The reality, however, is that trauma doesn't just happen beyond the borders of our campuses—it happens within our campus communities. More to the point, it sometimes happens *because* of our organizations.

The idea of our organizations being sources of trauma and actively creating trauma may seem a bit abstract, so let me offer a few examples. Consider an example where a graduate student's advisor is emotionally and verbally abusive. Perhaps there's even a pattern of the behavior over time, yet the faculty member remains in their position continuing to create harm seemingly without any meaningful interventions to prevent it from happening. The professor is creating the potential for trauma and the institutional inaction is allowing it to happen. Consider another example in which a university policy requires a student to describe the details of why they struggled academically as part of an appeal process. This example happened to a previous research participant of mine, SJ, who ultimately felt she needed to detail her experience of sexual assault to her financial aid office to maintain a scholarship that was in jeopardy because of her deteriorating grades following her traumatic experience. Institutional policy in this case is creating the possibility of new harm or re-traumatization for SJ. Consider another example in which a racially minoritized staff member is experiencing repeated microaggressions in their work environment and yet White colleagues remain resistant to conversations about the harm. Institutional actors are creating potential for trauma in this example, and it's likely that those actions are supported by institutional norms with the same denial mechanisms in place. These examples are just a few of the many I could offer and that you may even already be considering as you encounter this limited list.

For some, embracing the reality that our organizations and organizational actors are creators of trauma can be a difficult mental schema to fully understand and endorse. Yet, I think many of us who have spent time in student affairs can point to ways in which the institutions within which we're embedded are creating harm and trauma. It may be harder yet to consider that possibility closer to home—how are our immediate offices, areas, or individual practices creating possibilities for trauma production?

Disproportionate Climate of Risk Management and Litigation Fear

A phrase I've heard frequently during my time working in higher education is some version of "legal says we can't do that." I imagine that phrase is familiar to many others who work in postsecondary education writ large. In fact, I was in a meeting just yesterday where I learned a decision that had been made a couple of years ago that several of us disagreed with was driven in part by concern about pending litigation and that now that we were past that there was more appetite institutionally to revisit the initial proposals. In many ways, our movements and instincts in higher education organizations have increasingly been dictated by hyperattention to the potential of litigation, both real and imagined.

To be clear, we obviously must operate within the bounds of the law in higher education and student affairs professionals must understand the legal dimensions of their work. That's a must. What I'm talking about here is something different, which is that of institutional actions predominantly or exclusively driven by desires to minimize the risk of being sued. The truth is we haven't always been at this place in higher education to the degree to which we're experiencing it now. Sun (2020) notes 2010 as being a marker in time when we started to see a shift toward a "compliance-responsive approach" in higher education. The compliance approach represents increased organizational and individual energy and attention "toward risk avoidance over the previous interest in balancing the rights and responsibilities of students and colleges" (Sun, 2020, p. 181).

Sun (2020) highlights a couple of frequently discussed drawbacks to the compliance approach. First, a compliance approach has the capacity to flatten issues that require complexity. In other words, focusing narrowly on legal dimensions of an issue may mean creating challenges and complications for another. Second, this approach often means that leaders are making decisions based in fear, which can lead to impeded creativity as well as constraining options for students, faculty, and staff.

The compliance climate and fears of litigation impact trauma-informed practice in a variety of ways, but one that I want to highlight is the way in which a fear-based orientation may draw us away from what may be most supportive of those who have endured trauma. Mandatory reporting policies related to Title IX are a clear example of this tendency. Numerous researchers have demonstrated and sounded the alarm on the harmful potential of mandatory reporting policies at colleges and universities to survivors of sexual violence (e.g., Freyd, 2016; Gómez, 2021; Holland et al., 2021). Yet, even in times when the legal obligations of Title IX have not required blanket mandatory reporting policies, many institutions have overinterpreted the law to implement them. I would argue that institutions' desire to overinterpret is a product of understandably trying to simplify a difficult and complex landscape (i.e., it would take much more effort to piecemeal who is or isn't a mandatory reporter as opposed to more expansive interpretations that place everyone into that bucket) as well as concerns about litigation. Yet, there exist alternative interpretations of how to honor mandatory reporting requirements of Title IX through survivor-centric approaches such as those enacted at the University of Oregon that center on mandatory supporting (Freyd, 2016).

I'm a trauma scholar, not a legal scholar, so I'm not going to pretend I have advice to offer about how we need to interpret law. What I can offer is that there is harm done and threats to trauma-informed practice when our focus is exclusively on litigation minimization at the expense of remembering the experiences of real people in organizations who may be harmed by virtue of those decisions. At the very least, we need to be aware of the threats of fear-based decision-making in the face of real or imagined lawsuits and question the complicated ways that harm can travel. Harm needs to be considered for those members of the community who are impacted negatively by the fallout of an overemphasis on fear of lawsuits.

I want to end this section with a hopeful story that profoundly impacted me and remains a key "aha" moment in my career. When I was a master's student at the University of Maryland I did an internship in the student conduct office that was then under the direction of Dr. John Zacker. Although John wasn't my direct supervisor for my internship we had frequent opportunities to interact that summer and I relished 1:1 meetings with him where I could learn more about his approach to student conduct, which was highly developmental and student-centered. He also struck me as someone who was a strong advocate for his staff. In one of our meetings, John told me about the challenges that staff in conduct can face, because you're in these situations with students where sometimes you can imagine the potential lawsuit that could ensue or sometimes you have lawyers representing students already calling you with such threats. John told me that his message to staff was clear—he wanted them to work driven by what they believed to be the right thing to do on behalf of the student and community, rather than driven by fear about the possibility of a lawsuit. His expectation was that his staff knew the legal dimensions of their work and consulted with legal counsel when needed to inform their decisions, but ultimately he wanted their primary focus to be on doing what they perceived to be in the best interest of students, not merely avoiding a potential lawsuit.

I have come back to that perspective numerous times in my career and have shared that anecdote perhaps equally numerous times. I find that kind of leadership sadly refreshing. Too often I have encountered leaders in higher education paralyzed by hypothetical lawsuits and unwilling to do the right thing as a result. John, meanwhile, reminds me that there is space in our work to do what is right. That perspective takes boldness and often does not come without a different kind of risk, but in my estimation, we need more of that kind of decision-making in the current climate.

Discomfort-Resistant Leadership

The final barrier to trauma-informed practice that I want to highlight is subtle in many respects, yet fuels other practices that keep us away from truly trauma-informed practice, which is that of leaders actively resisting discomfort. In other words, leaders struggle with the important leadership skill of learning to find "comfort with being uncomfortable" (Kezar et al., 2021, p. 18). Trauma is inherently a difficult subject and narratives of trauma can be silenced in social spaces and discourses as a result (Okello & Shalka, 2022). Part of why hearing about others' traumas is resisted is because it brings up our own vulnerabilities in the world when we're made aware that bad things can and do happen to people we care about. It's not uncommon for people to feel uncomfortable about trauma and not really know what to do or how to respond. Yet, when leaders get stuck in this space and can't sit with things that are uncomfortable, significant barriers arise for trauma-informed practice.

How do we ask an organization to embrace knowledge about trauma and its difficulty when our leaders actively avoid topics and situations that require being with discomfort? These actions (or inactions) don't even have to be explicitly connected to trauma. For example, imagine a search process within a division and a debrief meeting in which someone wants to discuss issues related to perceived racist and sexist comments that came through feedback forms from colleagues about the candidates. Imagine a leader of that division shutting down the conversation and not providing a follow-up space to discuss the issue. The action could be driven by that leader's discomfort with what would be a challenging conversation for a division to have. But, that discomfort signals many things to those who may be experiencing similar harms in the environment including that this isn't a space committed to safety or harm reduction.

Leaders who seem challenged by sitting with the possibilities of trauma or difficult knowledges arising or are uncomfortable with multiple perspectives may be rooted in desires for control and stabilization. This is where, again, our work in trauma-informed environments becomes so deeply entwined with systems of power and oppression, because some of that active work of those in power to avoid discomfort is emblematic of White supremacy culture (Okun, 2021). On the other hand, as I mentioned previously, sometimes organizations and organizational actors are themselves traumatized in ways that make discomfort really challenging or even intolerable (Smith & Freyd, 2014), and leaders' instincts away from discomfort may be products of their own traumatization (for personal or professional reasons) that may result in their own deep needs to seek safety, predictability, and control. In short, these are complex issues and the behaviors we see on the surface frequently have much deeper roots that we need to both personally and organizationally unpack in the context of equity-minded trauma-informed practice. When we fully embrace and lean into some of these difficult realities and topics it can have a destabilizing effect in the interim (though I would argue there's a longer-term stabilizing effect as it creates space for the potential of truly trauma-informed work).

How Do We Get There?

In many previous chapters, the focus has been at the level of individual actions that support and promote trauma-informed practice. In this section, I'm moving up to a 30,000-foot view to imagine the kinds of strategies we need for trauma-informed practice to have a holistic and proactive infusion within a particular organizational context and culture. For many organizations, embracing trauma-informed practice means a culture shift. Although some of the ideas will have congruence and resonance with principles that have been discussed in other ways in this book, the sphere of influence connected to these ideas is broader and systemic. As you progress through the concepts that follow, sit with them in terms of how they can be used as lenses and practices to impact the system.

Invest in Education

If the theme of education being an essential building block of trauma-informed practice hasn't been obvious enough yet in this book, here it is again. I won't belabor previous points here, but I do want to emphasize some additional considerations and nuances relative to the role of education toward trauma-informed practice through an organizational and systems-level lens. First, as we envision an entire system, this bird's eye view gives us an opportunity to map out the various pockets and constituencies of any community to ensure we aim for broad coverage in providing information and education about trauma. The more people who have a deep understanding of trauma and its trajectories, the better we're able to function and support one another in trauma-informed ways. In many cases, trauma-informed efforts happen because of particular needs from a specific office in relation to their work (such as a conduct office or Title IX office), but at the systems level, we need to ensure that educational efforts are coordinated and intentional, with messages delivered in ways that are tailored to specific needs of different areas in our organizations. We can't just leave trauma-informed practice up to the champions who want to take it on as one of their own interests—we need divisional commitments to infuse trauma education into collective work.

A second point I want to make about education in a trauma-informed system relates to the importance of envisioning this work among an organization's leadership. Can trauma-informed practice be a grassroots effort? Certainly. But, there will inevitably be barriers to a system being truly trauma-informed if its leaders don't have a deep understanding of trauma and consequently work in ways to minimize harm and intentionally engage in equity and wellness-centric decision-making and practice. This means that leadership teams should be engaging in their own tailored educational work about trauma and specific conversations about what knowledge about trauma and its aftermath means for their practice. What does a trauma-informed approach ask of a director of residential life? Of an associate dean of students? Of a vice president for student affairs? These are the kinds of reflections and nuances of practice that should be engaged both by individual leaders and by leadership teams as they envision what trauma-informed practice entails in their day-to-day responsibilities as well as visioning for the future. Trauma-informed practice is not just reactive to specific moments of trauma—it should be a lens leaders use to actively inform decision-making and conceptualizations of the work of leaders.

Use Wellness and Humanity as Guideposts for Decision-Making

I see trauma-informed work as important for a couple of reasons. First, we engage in this work to reduce the potential of creating new harms or re-traumatization of those who have already endured trauma. Second, we engage in this work to clear space for healing. In that clearing and holding space for healing, we simultaneously have the potential to envision new purposes for organizations. In essence, this work can help us imagine the future of organizations as rooted in equity, wellness, and healing. I find the thought exercise intoxicating to imagine the purpose of our work grounded in humanity and healing.

Trauma-informed practice is demanding (perhaps) different heuristics for decision-making in our organizations that prioritize wellness and humanity. I offer that these may be different ways of approaching our work, because there is much evidence that indicates how much existing student affairs practice is quite antithetical to wellness and humanity for faculty, staff, and students. Sallee's (2020) thought-provoking work to highlight how ideal worker norms operate in student affairs makes clear how our organizations function to support burnout rather than wellness. The ideal student affairs worker is someone who can devote themselves to their work ahead of personal needs and perform their student supporting roles without being emotionally impacted, a dehumanizing standard that promotes a machine rather than a person. A recent report released by ACPA (College Student Educators International) about twenty-first-century employment in higher education argues that White supremacy culture is a major contributor to burnout in student affairs and organizational inability to meet the holistic needs of staff (ACPA Presidential Task Force, 2022). They cite some of Okun's (2021) domains of White supremacy culture that are pervasive in higher education, including fear, perfectionism, urgency, quantity over quality, right to comfort, and urgency. Not only do these norms promote a culture that works against the aims of equity and wellness, but they also create conditions for re-traumatization in an organization.

Trauma-informed practice can be an antidote to these forms of organizational harm when we begin to view the practice as a humanizing one. To embody this kind of practice, we begin decision-making processes through the lens of wellness and the humanity of our colleagues and students. There are numerous examples of how we might put this lens to work (Shalka, 2022a). For example, we may do intentional work to slow down, which isn't something that we're particularly good at in higher education. Being intentional about creating a pause in our practice leaves space for the possibility that trauma is present in our interactions at the same time it works against the frenetic paces of neoliberal and White supremacy culture contexts that cause harm (Okun, 2021; Shalka, 2022a). This slowing down might mean leaving space to involve people in decisions that concern them rather than insisting on quick decisions that leave people out. It might mean leaving space for grief and disagreement, rather than insisting on environments with room only for toxic positivity. This might mean creating space for staff, students, and faculty to think and be rather than just do. This might mean actively taking items off a meeting agenda or creating mechanisms for staff to take time off or have meeting-free weeks. Using wellness and humanity as guideposts for decision-making is something accessible to us at any level of an organization, but it may mean trying out new ways of working. When wellness and humanity are used as guideposts for decision-making, our practices are firmly grounded in anti-oppressive practices that create space for wellness and belonging.

Audit Policy and Practice Through a Trauma Lens

I briefly shared an example earlier about one of my research participants, SJ, and her harmful interactions with her financial aid office related to her trauma. After being sexually assaulted, SJ began to struggle in her academics, and over time, her GPA was falling, putting a scholarship she was on in jeopardy. Her institution offered a way for her to appeal losing the scholarship, but to do so she had to write an essay to the financial aid office explaining why her grades had fallen. SJ was financially dependent on this scholarship and felt she had no choice but to plead her case to maintain it, which ultimately meant she was writing an essay about her sexual assault to nameless, faceless people she didn't know in the financial aid office. In many ways, that process mirrored the ways SJ had already been violated.

SJ's experience is one I talk about frequently in relation to trauma-informed practice, because it's one that perhaps could have been prevented if a trauma lens were present on policy and practice. Perhaps there could have been an alternate process or different language related to the policy in which SJ wouldn't have been compelled to bare the very vulnerable details of her experience in a way that produced additional harm.

Many examples like SJ's become apparent and problematic in hindsight, but proactive intentionality might allow us to imagine this scenario before it happens and then prevent it from happening. An important organizational approach to minimize traumatization and re-traumatization is that of very actively and intentionally auditing policies and practices through a trauma lens. This means that we start to evaluate our practice, policies, and decisions through a "what if?" lens, imagining what it might be like to interact with particular policies or practices if someone has endured various kinds of trauma (Shalka, 2022b). For example, we might ask hypothetical questions such as: What might it be like for a student who has experienced [particular kind of trauma] to have to meet with me? Or, what might it be like for a student who has experienced [particular kind of trauma] to encounter the language of this particular policy or communication from our office? Or, what might it be like for a student who has experienced [particular kind of trauma] to attend this event that I have planned?

Our intentional auditing through a trauma lens should also be conscious of the spaces in which we interact with students. We may consider the need for space audits where we look at the physical environment for ways in which it communicates safety or unsafety, belonging or exclusion (Shalka, 2022b). For example, glass walls communicated unsafety to one of my participants, Amira, who found a sense of safety with her back against opaque walls. Another one of my participants, Charlie, was left feeling completely destabilized and in a fetal position in a hallway after a professor showed a clip of a movie about sexual violence without providing the class with a warning about what was to happen.

Finally, our audits of policy and practices must also seek to map the ways in which trauma is created at our institutions (Shalka, 2022b). We might begin by documenting examples where students or colleagues have expressed being harmed within the context of our institutions. As Gorski (2020) offers, such incidents "rarely happen in isolation" (para. 23) and must be probed for some of the underlying belief systems that allow such incidents to occur and potentially perpetuate a network of similar harm. For example, if we identify examples of sexual violence or microaggressions, we might then follow up by asking questions such as: "What is it about the institutional culture of a school that allows this to happen?" and "What other traumas do we perpetuate by allowing [heterosexist, racist, ableist, sexist, etc.] cultures to persist?" (Gorski, 2020, para. 24).

Earnestly Improve the Campus Climate

Trauma happens in the context of systems of power and oppression, and issues of racism, sexism, ableism, etc. contribute to traumatization in varied ways (Shalka, 2022b). These systemic forms of oppression can be sources and/or amplifiers of trauma, which helps explain why campus climate is one contributor to why trauma survivors may feel a reduced sense of belonging in their campus communities (Shalka & Leal, 2022). Thus, our trauma-informed efforts at systems levels have to take very seriously our work to improve the campus climate for students of all social identities and backgrounds in relation to student trauma.

Work to improve campus climate isn't new in the portfolio of priorities for student affairs administrators, yet it's useful to see these aims as congruent with trauma-informed practice. Despite campus climate work as a priority in student affairs, there are numerous examples where we don't get it right, especially when it's attended to superficially or reactively. Far too often, concerns about campus climate for students, faculty, and staff arrive on the heels of a crisis. Kezar and Fries-Britt (2020) offer an example of a racial campus crisis and the ways that institutions so often get these moments wrong, because they fail to attend to the trauma, emotions, and long-term harm of systemic oppression. Instead, campuses often react by creating task forces, gathering some data, and writing reports. That's the problem. Our organizational machines know how to look busy in the face of injustice, but far too often miss the mark of engaging in real work and institutional change to impact how campus climate is experienced for the students, staff, and faculty who are primarily negatively impacted.

Real change related to campus climate is difficult because it requires that we change the status quo, and there are numerous mechanisms in place that keep that from happening. Current operating systems are of benefit to many people on a campus, particularly those who embody privileged social identities and statuses. In an episode of Student Affairs NOW (Pope, 2021), Dr. Carlton Green talks about the culture of nice that exists in higher education where we become consumed with keeping harmony and affirming people at the expense of being able to have real, honest conversations about the difficult things that we need to dig more deeply into, especially around issues of racism and other forms of oppression. That culture of nice is one mechanism that keeps the status quo in place. When Dr. Green was asked by host Dr. Raechele Pope how our campuses might be different if we were to wake up one day and a culture of nice was gone, he responded in the following way:

> We would actually be centering the experiences of the most marginalized people on our campuses. . . . We would actually really be talking about those and not only talking about those, but integrating those into how we think about our strategic planning for the institution.
>
> (Pope, 2021)

Addressing the roots of harmful campus climates means foregrounding the experiences of those who are being harmed (the most marginalized on the campus as Dr. Green's above quote suggests), and integrating those experiences and voices explicitly and fundamentally into planning and decision-making. I would guess that many if not most student affairs educators would agree that attention to campus climate is important (and perhaps after reading much of this book also realizing why it matters in a trauma-informed system). Yet, we seem to continue to witness consistent and familiar forms of harm on our campuses that suggest our best intentions don't quite cut it. This is congruent with what developmental psychologists Drs. Robert Kegan and Lisa Lahey (2009) learned in their research about change. In short, a desire to change is necessary for change to happen, but it is not sufficient. Rather, we need to excavate for the behaviors that work against our desired change and use those behaviors as pathways toward unearthing the even deeper underlying priorities, needs, and assumptions we hold that may work in contradiction to our stated goals.

As we think about the kind of systems-level work needed to cultivate trauma-informed student affairs practice, it includes gathering data and identifying solutions related to campus climate, but that is an insufficient endpoint. We must also have honest and deliberate practices to interrogate what assumptions and beliefs are at odds with our intentions to improve the campus climate. For example, we may be afraid of change, of losing control, or assume change needs to happen incrementally. Or, we may meet those who express harms occurring with doubt and/or animosity. We need to get at those deeper layers and beyond a culture of nice that upholds all the -isms that continue to define much of our work in higher education. In that honesty and cultural excavation, we have to then act and actually do. As Kezar and Fries-Britt (2020) make the case for, that action needs to be conceptualized as "doing with" (p. 93). In other words, our work to improve campus climate must be engaged by working with those who are primarily impacted by harm at our institution at the same time we work to amplify equity and justice work that is already making a positive impact.

Focus on Trust

In *Emergent Strategy*, Adrienne Maree Brown (2017) discusses *moving at the speed of trust* as a foundational principle to her approach and notes that our work in a system is strengthened by focusing on "critical connections more than critical mass" (p. 42). There's something so powerful about that perspective to me, in part because it pushes us away from the neoliberal logics that undergird many of our organizations (demanding us to focus on "more" as better), and instead reminds us that quality of connection and relationship is what matters. I also love this concept because it provides a clear compass for systems and institutional actors to consider in how to orient our trauma-informed work, which should be profoundly in the direction of relationships and trust.

Trust is something that can be severely compromised during experiences of trauma. Thus, it emerges as an important consideration for trauma-informed systems to create conditions of safety and support for those who have endured trauma. In fact, the Substance Abuse and Mental Health Services Administration (2014) lists "trustworthiness and transparency" as one of six principles deemed fundamental to a trauma-informed approach.

We must envision trust and transparency as having both proactive and reactive dimensions in the face of trauma. Certainly, organizations should be attentive to trust and transparency through the process of a Title IX complaint, for example, but envisioning our work in building trust and being transparent about our processes solely in the aftermath of trauma is misguided and honestly too late. Let me share an example to illustrate this point. Amira (one of my research participants) shared that she didn't feel she had anywhere to go on her campus in relation to her traumatic experiences. She knew the Title IX office was specifically to report harm in the form of sexual violence which wasn't her experience. As she considered where she could go, she struggled with being able to trust that she would be taken seriously. Here is how she articulated it:

> So again, it goes back to the validation and validity thing. . . . Are they going to believe me? For one. Are they going to justify it and take it

seriously? Are they going to actually look into it? But also, it's this concern of going to, because when you report something like that on a campus, they're more than likely going to involve a police office of some kind, and racial profiling exists, and my experiences with cops have not been ideal on or off campus. It's not ideal. So to involve them, like do I really want to kind of thing?

Amira shared experiences about being pulled over by campus police for having a license plate with the school mascot on it (something she was told by campus police wasn't allowed, but numerous other students had on their cars seemingly without incident) and being followed across campus by university police. She also told me stories of feeling she didn't have a space supportive of her identity as a Muslim woman on campus, feeling that even the diversity and equity office wasn't a place for her because it focused mostly on issues of race related to being White or Black. She also shared a troubling story about a friend who is trans* and was being harassed and bullied because of that identity in the context of a student group that Amira was a part of. Amira and another member tried to take their concerns to multiple places, including to upper-level administrators in their student affairs office only to have nothing done in support of their friend and feeling that those they were meeting with did not understand the harm.

What do Amira's collective experiences mean? They mean there was practically no trust in her institution established long before she may have needed assistance in relation to her trauma. In practice, this all contributed to exactly why she didn't seek help from people at her school. In essence, trust and transparency in the aftermath of trauma for a student are rather irrelevant if that student isn't even able to seek services and support on a campus because of the profound distrust already established.

Trauma-informed work must advance systems that ensure proactive trust and relationship-building with every student on a campus. This is a multifaceted project because trust is fostered and held both individually and collectively. Our trust is earned through the very small and large actions and inactions we engage in as student affairs professionals situated in units and departments across an institution.

Mundell (2022) shares a poignant story of his work as a senior student affairs professional encountering many students who shared versions of a similar theme with him—"You're only meeting with me because you're paid to listen" or "You're only meeting with me because you don't want the institution to look bad." Mundell offers that much of his learning curve toward being more trauma-informed meant his attention to connecting with students as human beings, and that translated to intentionally building rapport as a building block toward establishing trust as he began to ask himself the question "Why would this student believe that I cared for them and how can I demonstrate that I truly do?" (Mundell, 2022, p. 22). That demonstration needed to come from a place of authentic care. As Mundell concludes, "Trauma-informed practice is not about convincing someone that you care, but rather, demonstrating that their personhood has value to you beyond their status as a student or your status as a professional hired to intervene to ensure their safety" (p. 22). What would it mean for us to think about the systematic structures and mechanisms that can be put in place to demonstrate to every student our sense of their value and our investment in building a relationship with them and working toward earning their trust?

Foster Institutional Courage

I want to end this chapter by discussing a powerful concept based in the work of Dr. Jennifer Freyd. Earlier in this chapter, I discussed her work on institutional betrayal as a barrier to trauma-informed practice (Smith & Freyd, 2013). What I appreciate so much about her career is that she was able to illustrate what's not working at the same time her research has presented alternatives of what can make a difference. The powerful antidote that Dr. Freyd offers is that of *institutional courage* (Freyd, 2018).

A provocatively titled article in *the Chronicle of Higher Education* captures the challenges we're facing in higher education related to sexual violence specifically (but arguably trauma broadly) and how Dr. Freyd's work might present a roadmap forward: *Why are colleges so cowardly?: Jennifer Freyd has a few ideas* (Bartlett, 2021). What Dr. Freyd offers is that colleges and universities are resistant to change away from acts of institutional betrayal because it involves reconfigurations of power. She is quoted in the article as saying:

> Somehow these systems, without individuals necessarily realizing it, develop these ways to preserve the status quo. And I know this has something to do with power because when you're trying to change the system, you're asking for some shift in power.
>
> (Bartlett, 2021, para. 2)

The concept of institutional courage requires a bit of a paradigm shift for many institutions to push beyond the conscious and unconscious ways our systems work to maintain the status quo. Freyd's (2018) institutional courage framework includes ten principles, but I want to emphasize three components here that I see as asking institutional actors to adopt stances of humility that are discouraged in systems built around values of White supremacy and desires for perfection and rights to comfort (Okun, 2021). The three principles I emphasize here include: (1) bear witness, be accountable, and apologize; (2) make sure leadership is educated about research on sexual violence and related trauma (and by extension I will add trauma broadly); and (3) cherish the whistleblower (Freyd, 2018).

The bearing witness principle insists on institutions creating space for individuals who are harmed to talk about what has happened (Freyd, 2018). Then, it takes that work a step further to demand that institutions admit the mistakes they have made in relation to that harm and apologize when that has happened. How powerful is that? I can think of examples of inspiring leaders I've worked with who model that kind of behavior and the transformative impacts it has on the organization as a humanizing space. Unfortunately, I can think of far too many examples of watching leaders engage in opposite behavior where there is maneuvering to hide and conceal or minimize harm that has happened and true difficulties in sitting with things that are uncomfortable.

The education principle is congruent with the education theme that has appeared throughout this book. We need leaders to understand what trauma is and how it unfolds to be better supports to those who have survived it. I mention it again here to show how that point emerges in numerous places related to trauma, but also because I see it as an act of humility. There are many ways we place our leaders in boxes of needing to be experts and know everything and have it figured out. Thus, it can be a place of humility and vulnerability to admit there are still things to learn.

Finally, I am ending with the principle that I have witnessed Dr. Freyd emphasize when she talks about institutional courage and it is also the one that I see as representing a truly profound paradigm shift in many of our systems—cherish the whistleblower (Freyd, 2018). As Dr. Freyd states of whistleblowers in relation to the organizations of which they are a part, "they're often the most loyal people" (Bartlett, 2021, para. 9). This is such a transformative practice for us to embrace in higher education where we can shift from seeing those who bring forward concerns and issues as the problem and instead begin to view them through the lens of those who are invested in the success of the organization. Whistleblowers are our superpower to help us improve toward being a more trauma-informed organization.

Conclusion

This chapter re-oriented us to the ultimate goal of trauma-informed work, which is that of creating organizations that are centered on wellness, equity, and care through the lens of knowledge about trauma. There are many existing structures and mechanisms rooted in the neoliberal logics of higher education that work against these goals, but we can engage in intentional work to transform those practices. That intentional work will include the kind of courage Dr. Freyd encourages and the deliberate listening and attention to pain that Adrienne Maree Brown advises.

References

ACPA Presidential Task Force on 21st Century Employment in Higher Education. (2022). *Report on 21st century employment in higher education.* ACPA College Student Educators International. https://drive.google.com/file/d/1Ij5YNqi5Nqiu-bSUmnDfqiYiOKlj3C2o/view

Bartlett, T. (2021, August 6). Why are colleges so cowardly? Jennifer Freyd has a few ideas. *The Chronicle of Higher Education.* https://www.chronicle.com/article/why-are-colleges-so-cowardly

Brown, A. M. (2017). *Emergent strategy: Shaping change, changing worlds.* AK Press.

Freyd, J. J. (2016, December 1). Required supporting instead of required reporting: Responding well to disclosures of campus sexual violence. *HuffPost.* https://www.huffpost.com/entry/required-supporting-instead-of-required-reporting-responding_b_5831d0d1e4b0d28e552150c3

Freyd, J. J. (2018, January 11). When sexual assault victims speak out, their institutions often betray them. *The Conversation.* https://theconversation.com/when-sexual-assault-victims-speak-out-their-institutions-often-betray-them-87050

Gómez, J. M. (2021, June 8). *Reforming title IX: Evidence of harm of universal mandated reporting for marginalized survivors of campus sexual violence.* https://titleixdoelivehearingsgomez2021.blogspot.com/2021/06/reforming-title-ix-evidence-of-harm-of.html

Gorski, P. (2020). How trauma-informed are we, really? *Educational Leadership, 78*(2), 14–19. https://www.ascd.org/el/articles/how-trauma-informed-are-we-really

Holland, K. J., Hutchison, E. Q., Ahrens, C., & Torres, M. G. (2021). Reporting is not supporting: Why mandatory supporting, not mandatory reporting, must guide university sexual misconduct policies. *Proceedings of the National Academy of Sciences of the United States of America, 118*(52). https://doi.org/10.1073/pnas.2116515118

Kegan, R., & Lahey, L. L. (2009). *Immunity to change: How to overcome it and unlock potential in yourself and your organization.* Harvard Business Press.

Kezar, A., & Fries-Britt, S. (2020). Navigating a campus racial crisis: Building capacity, leading through trauma and the recovery process. *Change: The Magazine of Higher Learning, 52*(2), 89–93. https://doi.org/10.1080/00091383.2020.1732795

Kezar, A., Holcombe, E., Vigil, D., & Dizon, J. P. M. (2021). *Shared equity leadership: Making equity everyone's work.* American Council on Education, University of Southern California, Pullias Center for Higher Education. https://www.acenet.edu/Documents/Shared-Equity-Leadership-Work.pdf

Mundell, C. (2022). Doing no harm: One practitioner's journey towards trauma-informed practice. In T. R. Shalka & W. K. Okello (Eds.), *Trauma-informed practice in student affairs: Multidimensional considerations for care, healing, and wellbeing* (New Directions for Student Services, Vol. 177, pp. 17–25). Wiley. https://doi.org/10.1002/ss.20411

Okello, W. K., & Shalka, T. R. (2022). Introduction to trauma-informed practice in student affairs. In T. R. Shalka & W. K. Okello (Eds.), *Trauma-informed practice in student affairs: Multidimensional considerations for care, healing, and wellbeing* (New Directions for Student Services, Vol. 177, pp. 7–15). Wiley. https://doi.org/10.1002/ss.20410

Okun, T. (2021). *White supremacy culture—still here.* https://drive.google.com/file/d/1XR_7M_9qa64zZ00_JyFVTAjmjVU-uSz8/view

Pope, R. (Host). (2021, October 20). Canceling the culture of nice in higher education. *Student Affairs NOW* [Audio podcast episode No. 66]. https://studentaffairsnow.com/cultureofnice/

Pope, R. (Host). (2022, May 11). Trauma-informed practice. *Student Affairs NOW* [Audio podcast episode No. 97]. https://studentaffairsnow.com/trauma-informed/

Sallee, M. W. (2020). *Creating sustainable careers in student affairs: What ideal worker norms get wrong and how to make it right.* Stylus.

Shalka, T. R. (2022a). How a trauma-informed organization would change the face of higher education (and why we need it now more than ever). *Change: The Magazine of Higher Learning, 54*(4), 4–10. https://doi.org/10.1080/00091383.2022.2078148

Shalka, T. R. (2022b). Nurturing a trauma-informed student affairs division. *About Campus, 27*(2), 18–25. https://doi.org/10.1177/10864822221100253

Shalka, T. R., & Leal, C. C. (2022). Sense of belonging for college students with PTSD: The role of safety, stigma, and campus climate. *Journal of American College Health, 70*(3), 698–705. https://doi.org/10.1080/07448481.2020.1762608

Smith, C. P., & Freyd, J. J. (2013). Dangerous safe havens: Institutional betrayal exacerbates sexual trauma. *Journal of Traumatic Stress, 26,* 119–124. https://doi.org/10.1002/jts/21778

Smith, C. P., & Freyd, J. J. (2014). Institutional betrayal. *American Psychologist, 69*(6), 575–587. https://doi.org/10.1037/a0037564

Substance Abuse and Mental Health Services Administration [SAMHSA]. (2014). *SAMHSA's concept of trauma and guidance for a trauma-informed approach* (HHS Publication No. (SMA) 14-4884). Substance Abuse and Mental Health Services Administration. https://ncsacw.samhsa.gov/userfiles/files/SAMHSA_Trauma.pdf

Sun, J. C. (2020). An examination of anti-sexual harassment policies and practices: Legal administration for socially conscious campuses. In A. Kezar & J. Posselt (Eds.), *Administration for social justice and equity in higher education: Critical perspectives for leadership and decision-making* (pp. 176–195). Routledge.

Venet, A. S. (2021). *Equity-centered trauma-informed education.* W. W. Norton & Company.

8

TOWARD A TRAUMA-INFORMED STUDENT AFFAIRS PRACTICE

April: So in the study, do you get to say the school that the [participants] went to?
Tricia: I don't just to help protect anonymity.
April: That's so sad. So you never get to know whose schools are good.
Tricia: I know. Because your school sounds like the place that would be a perfect case study of how it should be.
April: I know, right?

April and I had covered a lot of ground together by the final moments of our last interview. We had chronicled moments of devastation and difficulty while she was a college student in relation to her mother's murder. I recall leaving our first interview together and just sitting down to cry—the depth of the pain and overwhelm she had to confront was more than anyone should have to endure, college student or not. However, our time together also left me knowing that the essence of enduring traumatic experiences is not pain alone. It often also includes elements of resilience, possibility, and connection, characteristics that were certainly indicative of April and her experience.

In the above excerpt from our final interview, April was expressing a sense of gratitude to have been at the institution that she was at when her traumatic experience occurred. Right before that excerpt, she lamented the fact that she knows other students are struggling with trauma in places where they don't have access to the kind of support system at their institutions that she had. She wished there

DOI: 10.4324/9781003444435-9

was a way for her institution to be known, I think, because she was hoping others could learn from her school how to do right by trauma survivors.

As I shared with April, my commitment to anonymity as a researcher means I can't tell the world April's school. But, what I can do because of what I've learned from participants like April over the years is offer a toolkit to student affairs educators about what it takes to create the kinds of trauma-informed environments that are supportive of the recuperation of a student like April. I can also expand that possibility out even further to help student affairs professionals consider their roles in trauma-informed systems in terms of not only supporting survivors of trauma directly but also in creating the kinds of conditions that contribute to envisioning and enacting equity and wellness-centric organizations that benefit all members of a campus community.

I want to return to a thought exercise I mentioned in the previous chapter: *What would it look like to work and/or study in a truly trauma-informed organization? What would it feel like?* What arises for you as you sit with those questions now after moving through this book?

In previous chapters, I outlined many strategies and components that are part of working toward a trauma-informed student affairs practice. This work starts and continues through the vehicle of education—the more staff, faculty, and students on any college campus who understand what trauma is and how it impacts individuals and communities, the better the support we can expect trauma survivors will receive. However, education is a necessary, but insufficient condition of a trauma-informed system. While the education piece may inform our work, we then need specific strategies and ways of being to actually create trauma-informed systems. In other words, we need to not just know something about trauma but actually do something with that knowledge.

At the individual level, much of our work in trauma-informed systems happens through how we move through the world and interact with others. I offered three ways of being to help frame our energies to this end including: nurturing a sense of humanness (for ourselves and others); seeing those impacted by trauma as whole beings; and arriving with compassionate curiosity.

In our work with students, we find ourselves supporting those who have directly experienced trauma, but also training and supporting student leaders who will, themselves, be working with student survivors. Inevitably, there are reactive dimensions to how we support both student survivors and student leaders, but we must envision proactive work too. I offered six specific practices for supporting student survivors of trauma, including nurturing relationships; being present; addressing issues of safety and control; attending to the complications of disclosure; providing resources and support mindfully; and holding space for growth, resilience, and recuperation. Meanwhile, as we think about working with student leaders and paraprofessionals who will also be exposed to the trauma of their peers, we can envision our work in terms of both proactive elements (such as teaching student leaders about trauma and preparing them for what might happen when they're exposed to trauma), as well as the necessary reactive elements of supporting them after trauma exposure. A key point I emphasized is also our collective need as a profession and individual professionals to both trouble and challenge our conscious and unconscious framings of student leaders and paraprofessionals as superhuman.

We then have to pan out to the 30,000-foot view and consider how our systems are contributing to harm or harm reduction in the context of building a trauma-informed organization. The ultimate goal of trauma-informed practice is equity-focused systems of wellness and care. To get there we need to invest in education; use wellness and humanity as guideposts for decision-making; audit policy and practice through a trauma lens; earnestly improve the campus climate; focus on trust; and foster institutional courage.

So, *what would it look like and what would it feel like to work and/or study somewhere that was enacting all these things as well as other details presented in this book?* What would it mean for your own campus to create conditions supportive of a student like April in her recuperation? What would it take for a student to know that you care not because it's your job but because you value them as a human (Mundell, 2022)? What would it take for your organization as a whole to operate in a way that communicated that same message systemically?

As you sit further with these questions, take a few moments to document your thoughts and feelings. What tangibles and intangibles are present in that kind of environment for you and the students and colleagues with whom you work? What feelings arise for you imagining that environment?

Examine that list of thoughts and feelings you generated and consider your sphere of influence. What are the things you can do to help create that kind of environment? You might consider that sphere of influence both in terms of (a) your personal interactions and (b) your capacity to influence the system within which you work. For example, how might you create the kind of trauma-informed environment you imagined through your personal interactions? It might include the ways you show up with others, how you support students, or how you take care of yourself. How might you create the kind of trauma-informed environment you imagined through your influences on your work system? It might include auditing the policies and practices that guide your work, working as a leader who develops a capacity to sit with discomfort, planning educational programs about trauma, running meetings in ways that foster a sense of predictability and trust, or meeting with senior leaders to advocate for many of the practices described in this book.

The imperative for a trauma-informed student affairs practice could not be more clear. I shared in Chapter 2 about the prevalence of trauma in college communities with the vast majority of students arriving to their postsecondary institutions already having experienced trauma. That prevalence will grow—some students who have already been exposed to trauma will encounter additional trauma in college and others will face trauma for the first time. Our contemporary moment has made us freshly aware of the prevalence of trauma in our lives and communities as we've reckoned with a global pandemic, continued racial injustice, and ongoing gun violence in the United States. Students are struggling, but so are we as professionals supporting them and living amidst the same challenging contexts. The imperative could not be more clear.

A trauma-informed student affairs practice offers us a pathway forward—it represents our aspiration toward viewing our organizations not just as mechanisms to get things done but as humanizing spaces with transformative potential toward well-being and healing.

Students like April are depending on us.

Reference

Mundell, C. (2022). Doing no harm: One practitioner's journey towards trauma-informed practice. In T. R. Shalka & W. K. Okello (Eds.), *Trauma-informed practice in student affairs: Multidimensional considerations for care, healing, and wellbeing* (New Directions for Student Services, Vol. 177, pp. 17–25). Wiley. https://doi.org/10.1002/ss.20411

Index

ableism 8, 17, 27–28, 141
Angelou, Maya 9
Anzaldúa, Gloria 59

bearing witness 147
belonging 18, 37–39, 104
Beloved Community 63–64
body shaming 36, 70
boundaries 119–120
Brown, Adrienne Maree 98, 128, 144, 148
Brown, Brené 22, 80, 119
Brown, Laura 8
bullying 86, 145
burnout 54, 139

campus climate 37, 52, 91, 141–143, 153
campus shootings 44, 90
classism 8, 27
cognitive development 25
college students: belonging and community 18, 37–39, 104; identity of 25, 29, 31–32; invalidation of 69; negotiations in the environment 34–37; relationships of 32–34, 52, 85–87; as trauma survivors 22–39, 73; as veterans 43; *see also* student leaders
community 37–39
compassion 68, 80
compassionate curiosity 62, 65–68, 152
compassion fatigue 119

conscious referrals 95
content/trigger warnings 92
COVID-19 pandemic 44, 60
Crenshaw, Kimberlé 42
culture of nice 142
cultures of care 53–54

Diagnostic and Statistical Manual of Mental Disorders (*DSM-5*) 10–11
disclosure 92–94
discomfort-resistant leadership 135–136
discrimination 36, 42, 70, 86

education: about trauma 115–117, 147–148, 152; investment in 137–138
empathy 2, 22, 32, 34, 86, 119
equity 39, 43, 49–50, 69–70, 87, 91, 128–129, 136–139, 143, 145, 148, 152, 153
Erikson, Kai 2, 86
Exercises: breathing exercise 79; grounding practice 79–80; visualization for putting in a box 121; visualization for releasing 120
expert companionship 99

fight/flight/freeze response 9–10
forced disclosure 93–94
Freyd, Jennifer 102–103, 130, 146–147, 148

INDEX

gender issues 15, 30
Germer, Christopher 68
Green, Carlton 142

harm: to community 15; concealing/minimizing 77, 115, 147; contributing to 29, 42, 45, 46, 51, 56, 61, 73, 76, 90, 92, 94–97, 117, 119, 127, 130–132, 134, 140, 153; and institutional betrayal 102–103; long-term 142; microaggressions as 132; organizational 139, 141, 143; prevention of 75; reduction of 46, 50, 52, 53–54, 57, 68, 136, 153; reporting 144; unawareness of 131
healing 128, 138
healing centered engagement 65
hegemonic masculinity 27–28, 30
heterosexism 141
humanness 62–64, 152
humbleness 67–68
humor, space for 125–126
hyperarousal 11–12, 44
hypervigilance 11–12, 72
hypoarousal 11–13, 44

identity: of college students 25, 29, 31–32; gender 29–30; group 29–30; racial 29–30; social 30, 70, 141, 142; social constructions of 26, 29–30
inequity 49
institutional betrayal 102–103, 130–131, 146–147
institutional courage 146–148, 153
interconnectivity 109
intersectionality 42

justice work 143

Kegan, Robert 143
King, Martin Luther Jr. 63–64
knowledge building 52–53, 57, 68–71; teaching about trauma 115–117

Lahey, Lisa 143
litigation fear 132–135

mandatory reporting policies 90, 102, 133
mandatory supporting policies 102, 134
masculinity, hegemonic 27–28, 30
Maté, Gabor 6, 90
mattering 103–106
Menakem, Resmaa 6

microaggressions 132, 141
Mundell, Chris 96–97

oppression 8, 26–28, 30, 49, 51–52, 57, 63, 139, 141, 142; systemic 16
orientation leaders (OLs) 110; *see also* student leaders

peer advisors 110; *see also* student leaders
peer mentorship 125
Platinum Rule 63
play, space for 125–126
posttraumatic growth (PTG) 98–99
posttraumatic stress disorder (PTSD) 10–11, 16, 24, 30, 37, 43, 72, 104
potentially traumatic events (PTEs) 7
predominantly White institutions (PWIs) 130
privilege 26–28, 30, 70, 142
psychological first aid (PFA) 122–124

racism 8, 17, 27, 42, 43–44, 49, 52, 141, 142
railway spine concept 16
recuperation 98–100
relationships 32–34, 52; nurturing 85–87; and trust 144
Remen, Rachel Naomi 83
resident assistants (RAs) 110–112, 114–115, 118, 125; *see also* student leaders
resilience 98–100
re-traumatization 43, 44–45, 46, 48, 53, 102, 117, 139
risk management 132–135

safety: addressing issues of 153; on campus 37, 52, 97, 114, 136; and control 47, 71, 72, 85, 90–92, 106, 153; creating conditions of 36, 48, 53, 117, 123, 124, 141, 144, 146; lack of 12; physical 6, 48; in relationships 34, 87; sense of 48; space for 43, 44; threats to 8
savior mentality 66
secondary traumatic stress 71–73, 116, 119, 121
self-advocacy 118
self-authorship 25
self-awareness 118
self-care 54, 73–74; breathing 79; connecting with others 80; emotional 78; importance of 74–77; mental 77;

physical 77; reconnecting with your body 79–80; social 77; SOS 78–80; spiritual 77–78; strategies of 77–78
self-protection 90
sexism 8, 17, 27, 42, 141
sexual assault 111–112, 119, 132, 140
sexual violence 11, 17–18, 24, 26, 27, 90–91, 102–103, 130, 133, 141, 144, 146, 147; experience of 32; perceptions of 28–29
shadow space 34–35
shell shock 16
silence 89
silencing 23–24, 29, 38, 71
skill building 68–71
social discourses 26, 28–29
social justice 49
sociogram exercise 87
space audits 92
Steinem, Gloria 4–5
Stevens, Maurice 15–17
stress 13, 90
Student Affairs NOW 129, 142
student leaders 28, 57, 81; dangers of superhuman construction 112–115; definitions of 110; as peer educators/paraprofessionals 110–112; peer mentorship for 125; personal limits of 118–120; psychological first aid (PFA) for 122–124; supporting trauma survivors 109; training and support for 115–126, 153; *see also* college students
Substance Abuse and Mental Health Services Administration (SAMHSA) 5, 48, 144
suicide 97, 114, 122

Title IX 133–4, 144
trauma: childhood 24; definitions of 2, 4–7, 11, 38; difficult-to-hear 100–101; "does it count?" 15–19; event-based 1, 36; experience of 1–2, 17–18; historical 8, 15, 27; intergenerational 8, 15, 27; multidimensionality of 13–15, 26; physical 13–14; psychological 7–8, 13–14; racial 8, 10, 26, 27, 51, 90; responses to 8–13; sources of 7–8, 131–132; subjective nature of 4, 19; teaching about 115–117; vicarious 72
trauma exposure response 72–73
trauma-informed practice 42–43, 57; being present 88–90; countering organizational harm 139; deficit-focused 65; definitions of 2, 44–48, 128, 146; developing knowledge and skills 68–71; equity-centered 49–50, 136–137; focus on building relationships and community 86–87; holistic approach to 49, 50–51, 57, 64–65; impact of 59–61; importance of 43–44; models of 48–54; organizational barriers to 129–136; principles of 48–9; putting into practice 54–55; in student affairs 50–54, 142–143, 153–154; thinking individually and systemically 55–56; underinvolvement vs. over-involvement 95–96; as way of being 61–68
trauma literature 30
trauma psychology 102, 130
trauma survivors: being present for 88–90; college students as 22–39; complexities of supporting 100–103; and the complications of disclosure 92–94; experience of 14, 23; listening to 23, 83, 89–90, 123–124; mattering to others 103–106; need to distance self from others 33–34; preparing student leaders to work with 117–121; resources for 95–98; re-traumatization of 43, 44–45, 46, 48, 53, 102, 117, 139; silencing of 23–24, 29, 38; space for growth, resilience, and recuperation 98–100; struggles of 17–18; support for 2, 32–33, 45, 46–48, 71–72, 83–106, 152; as whole beings 62, 64–65, 152
traumatic neurosis 16
traumatic recovery 28, 65
traumatization: discounting and contesting of 16–17; effect on the brain 14; responses to 8–13
triggering 6, 35, 36–37, 44, 61, 67, 74, 89, 91, 94, 95, 101–102, 112, 118; personal triggers 101–102
trigger warnings 92
trust 48, 80, 84, 86, 88, 130, 144–146, 153, 154

unsafety 35, 68, 125, 141

van der Kolk, Bessel 9, 13, 14
van Dernoot Lipsky, Laura 72
Venet, Alex Shevrin 49
victim blaming 24

INDEX

violence: gender-based 51; gun 44; hate-based 27; *see also* sexual violence
visualization 120–121

ways of being 61–68, 71; arriving with compassionate curiosity 65–68; nurturing a sense of humanness 62–64; seeing those impacted by trauma as whole beings 64–65

wellness-centered decision-making 53–54, 57, 80–81, 138–139, 153
"what else might be going on?" 39, 67, 71
whistleblowers 148
White House Task Force to Protect Students from Sexual Assault 43
White supremacy 136, 139, 147
women, stereotypes of 30

For Product Safety Concerns and Information please contact our EU
representative GPSR@taylorandfrancis.com
Taylor & Francis Verlag GmbH, Kaufingerstraße 24, 80331 München, Germany

www.ingramcontent.com/pod-product-compliance
Lightning Source LLC
Chambersburg PA
CBHW071411300426
44114CB00016B/2263